A MOLLY MAGUIRE STORY

BY PATRICK CAMPBELL

Published by

P.H. Campbell
82 Bentley Avenue
Jersey City, NJ 07304
(201) 434-2432

Printed in the United States of America
by
Princeton University Press
3175 Princeton Pike
Lawrenceville, NJ 08648

Cover Design by Robert T. Baker

Dedicated to Eileen, Padraic and Nora

PREFACE

On June 21, 1877, ten Irish-Americans were executed in the mining areas of Pennsylvania. All were accused of being members of a terrorist group called the Molly Maguires, and all were convicted of planning and carrying out the murder of a number of mining officials. Ten more Irish-Americans were executed in Pennsylvania in the next 18 months on the same charges. One of the men executed on June 21, 1877, was Alexander Campbell, grand-uncle of the author.

The Molly Maguire executions generated a great deal of controversy in Pennsylvania from the 1870s to the present, with Irish-Americans claiming the Mollies were framed by the mine owners, while other ethnic groups believe that they were guilty as charged and deserved the punishment they received.

The author first heard about the execution of his grand-uncle back in the late 1940s in Dungloe, County Donegal, Ireland, and in the early 1970s, while living in New Jersey, began a fifteen-year investigation into the entire Molly Maguire controversy in order to determine if Alexander Campbell was guilty or innocent.

A Molly Maguire Story is an account of that investigation.

INTRODUCTION

In order to comprehend all aspects of the trial and execution of Alec Campbell it is important to understand the environment that Campbell lived in in the coal regions of Pennsylvania during the 1860s and 1870s. The political, social and cultural environment bears little resemblance to the environment that exists there today.

During the period from 1860 to 1870, the coal mining industry went through a rapid expansion with the number of mine workers rising from 25,000 in 1860 to 53,000 in 1870. The Irish comprised one-third of all mine workers and their numbers exceeded the combined numbers of Welsh and English mine workers in the region.

The Irish were a disliked ethnic group in the area who were discriminated against because of their nationality and their religion. They were also intensely disliked, because, unlike other foreign workers in the area, they did not keep a low profile. Instead, they were assertive, outgoing, and inclined to fight back against anyone who tried to discriminate against them. Confrontations between Welsh and Irish occurred frequently.

Some of the huge mining companies in Pennsylvania were owned by English stockholders, who in turn appointed their American cousins -- white Anglo-Saxon Protestants -- as the top officials in their American holdings.

These WASPs in turn imported Welsh and English miners to work the coal mines as contract workers who were paid by the ton of coal mined, and the Welsh and English miners in turn hired laborers, mainly Irish, at a salary only a fraction of what the miners received.

The superintendents at many mines were Welsh, though sometimes English, and these superintendents saw to it that when a choice miner position opened up a Welshman or an Englishman got the job. These superintendents also had the power to hire and fire laborers and any Irishman who complained about the system was blacklisted and could not get a job at all.

The Irish who poured into the mining areas of Pennsylvania in the 1860s were refugees from the great Irish famine of the late 1840s. Some had stopped off in Boston or New York for a number of years before coming to Pennsylvania to seek a better life; others had come directly from Ireland.

Alec Campbell had come directly from Donegal to Pennsylvania in 1868. He had survived the catastrophic famine of the 1840s that had left more than half of his parish in Donegal dead of hunger and he was bitter about the horrors he had experienced back at home.

Most of the land in West Donegal was owned by absentee English landlords, and the agents who managed the estates were Welsh, English or Scots. Even as their tenants died on the roadsides of Donegal from hunger, the landlords had continued to demand grain from their tenants as rent -- or else they would evict them -- and this grain was shipped out of Burtonport, County Donegal, to Britain even as Alec Campbell's neighbors and relatives died of hunger. Only the assistance provided by English and Irish Quakers prevented the annihilation of the entire population.

Alec Campbell fled to America to find a better life, but he was not too happy to discover on his arrival in Pennsylvania that he had not left the old English-Welsh-Scots power structure behind him as he had imagined.

In their early years in Pennsylvania, the Irish congregated in settlements like Cass Township and Summit Hill, where they made up the majority of the population. In other towns, whole neighborhoods were Irish, and even if they were in the minority, they were not a silent minority and they always made their presence known.

The first major controversy that involved the Irish erupted in 1863, when President Lincoln's new conscription laws generated widespread opposition all over the country.

It was ironic that a president who is best remembered for his stand on civil rights for blacks should have approved a conscription law which penalized poor whites, but that is exactly what the law did -- allow the middle class or the wealthy to be exempt from service in the armed forces if they paid $300. The Irish viewed the draft as a violation of their civil rights -- because few of them had $30 to their name, never mind $300 -- and huge anti-draft riots broke out all over the country and involved the poor of other nationalities as well as the Irish.

Mining baron Franklin Gowen and the Pinkertons would claim in 1876 that the draft riots in Schuylkill County in 1863 were masterminded by the Molly Maguires, but this is hardly true, because there were huge draft riots in New York in the same year, which left hundreds dead and also involved the Irish, and no one has ever suggested that these riots were inspired by any group named the Molly Maguires.

General Charles Albright, who would later become chief prosecutor of Alec Campbell, was appointed by Lincoln to keep law and order in the

3

rebellious mining areas and he had his first confrontation with Irish mine workers in 1863 and was forced to back off.

He had led a military force into Schuylkill County to enforce the draft, but backed off when he was confronted by thousands of armed Irish laborers, among them Jack Kehoe. He would neither forgive or forget the insult offered him by the Irish, and he would take revenge 15 years later, when he helped send Kehoe to the gallows.

The political life of the area was dominated by Democrats and Republicans. Both parties represented capitalist interests and neither had Irish Catholics in its top echelons.

The Welsh and English usually voted Republican and the Irish usually voted Democratic.

The Welsh and English miners were in favor of freeing the black slaves in the South and were not afraid of them taking their jobs, which they believed were protected by British interests. So they supported Republican policies to free the slaves. The Welsh and the English were openly racist, however, and their support for the anti-slavery policy did not mean they accepted blacks as equals.

The Irish had nightmares of millions of freed blacks coming up from the South and displacing them in the mines as laborers, and so they joined the Democrats, who were opposed to Lincoln's anti-slavery policies. The Irish, however, in doing so, were no more racist than their Welsh or English neighbors.

The biggest newspaper in the area was the *Miner's Journal*, owned by Welsh-American Benjamin Bannan, who openly catered to the prejudices of the Welsh and English miners, and occasionally to the interests of the mine owners.

Bannan was a Protestant fundamentalist who despised the Catholic Church and openly berated the Irish as violent, uncivilized drunks. He wrote that the only thing the Irish were good at was opening saloons in the area and hanging out in them, and it was he who first began to blame the Irish for all the crime in the area. Later, he would begin to write about a secret organization he called the Molly Maguires, and it was he more than any other person who created the legend of the Molly Maguires.

There is no question that there was a great deal of crime in both Carbon and Schuylkill counties in the 1860s and 1870s and that the Irish were involved in it -- in riots, arson, sabotage and murder.

A survey of crime statistics, before the Molly Maguire era and after the Molly Maguire era, however, indicates clearly that the crime rate in the

4

area was as high before the Molly Maguire era as it was during the era and the crime rate did not drop after twenty alleged Mollies were executed and hundreds more were sent to jail. So, there was no correlation between the Molly era and increased crime.

Furthermore, as Walter Coleman reveals in his 1935 book on the Molly Maguires, a survey of crime statistics in other coal mining areas in the United States during this period, in areas that had few Irish workers shows a similar level of crime. The conclusion one must draw is that crime was an outcome of the mining environment, not of the lawlessness of any one ethnic group.

However, Bannan did not inform his readers of this, and the copies of the *Miners Journal* printed during this period would have you believe a horrendous crime wave was occurring and that the Ancient Order of Hibernians -- or the Molly Maguires -- was behind it.

Naturally, Irish laborers working the mines hated Bannan and his *Miners Journal* and considered it a biased newspaper.

* * * *

When John Siney formed the Workers Benevolent Association, the miners union, in 1868, he tried to merge the interests of Welsh and English miners and Irish laborers but without a great deal of success. However, when Gowen came on the scene the miners and the laborers were confronted with a common enemy who posed a threat to both, then the miners and the laborers began to cooperate -- though there was still no unity of interests.

Indeed, the small mine operators and the miners had greater interests in common than the miners had with other mine workers. Both the small mine operators and the miners had a vested interest in keeping the price of coal high. The miners were in reality small independent contractors who were paid a fixed rate per ton for the coal they mined, and the higher the price of coal the higher the wages they made. The small mine operators also made more money when the price of coal was high, and both the miners and the mine operators would cut production or even stop production in order to increase demand and maintain the price.

However, the rest of the mine workers, including the laborers, who were paid by the hour, gained little when the price of coal went up, and were badly hurt when there was a slow-down or a complete stoppage. Thus the mine laborers were at odds with the miners and the mine operators over this and a number of other issues.

The appearance of Franklin Gowen, Asa Packer and Charles Parrish on the scene changed a great deal of this. Gowen, Packer and Parrish headed railroad and coal companies whose financial health depended on increased production -- and therefore increased use of the railroads -- and these rail companies had bought up huge interests in coal mines in order to be able to control the freight shipped on the railroad.

Gowen's Reading Railroad, Packer's Lehigh Railroad, and Parrish's Lehigh & Wilkes Barre Coal Company were determined to ship as much coal out of the area as possible, thereby making quick profits for their companies, even though this glutted the market and the price of coal fell.

Siney of the WBA and Gowen got together and worked out an agreement which called for the miners to get an increase every time the price of coal went up, but no guaranteed base wage if coal went down, and Siney committed the union to this. But when the market became glutted and the price of coal fell, the miners saw their wages shrink by 50% and the laborers saw their wages go down to the point where they did not have enough money to feed their families even after working 60 hours a week.

Wildcat strikes followed against the coal mines owned by Gowen, Packer and Parrish and these strikes were led mainly by the Irish laborers, who were hardest hit by the recession.

Siney and most of the Welsh miners were opposed to strikes, because they believed that half a loaf was better than no bread. But the Irish laborers and some of the more disgruntled miners wanted a guaranteed wage from the mine owners and were determined to get it no matter what the cost.

The big mine owners used the chaotic conditions in the area to their own advantage. The small mine operators could not survive when they were faced with demands for higher wages on one hand and demands from the railroads for higher rail freight charges on the other, and when Gowen, Packer and Parrish dumped coal on the market from their own mines, the small mines went out of business one after another. The trio then bought up these mines at bargain-basement prices and added them to their collection.

By 1875, Gowen's Reading Company owned 40 mines with 9,000 employees and controlled the economy of Schuylkill and parts of Carbon counties. Parrish and his Lehigh & Wilkes Barre Coal Company had 14,000 employees and had a stranglehold on Luzerne and other parts of Carbon county. Packer owned Mauch Chunk and other huge holdings and was one of the three richest men in America.

Gowen, Packer, Parrish and the other major mining and business interests in the area decided that, while it was desirable to drive all small businessmen into bankruptcy, it would be suicidal to compete with one another.

So, in January 1873, Gowen, Parrish, Packer and a number of other mine owners and railroad moguls met in New York and fixed the price of coal wholesale. This was the first price-fixing cartel in American history.

The cartel also established quotas for each company's market share. Gowen's Reading got 25.85%, the Hudson got 18.37%, the Jersey Central got 16.15%, the Lehigh 15.95%, the Lackawanna 13.80% and Pennsylvania Coal Co. 9.85%.

The mine owners were now riding high. They had control of huge areas of the coal mining industry, which in turn guaranteed those who owned railroads that they would have a huge market share in shipping that coal out. They also had a stranglehold on the small mine operators in the area because they could charge them any price they choose for shipping their coal out, and this was gradually easing the small owners out.

But they were not able to control the Workers Benevolent Association -- especially the Irish element -- and they were determined to do something about that. They were not able to control the political arena in Schuylkill and Carbon counties either, even though they practically owned both counties, again because the Irish -- prodded by the AOH -- had switched their support from the Democratic candidates to Republican candidates who won many offices, including the governorship. The mine owners were determined to do something about the AOH also.

Gowen had ambitions that went beyond being a major player in the coal mining areas of Carbon and Schuylkill counties. He was determined to eventually gain a complete monopoly on the coal mining, distribution, and transportation network and to become a major power in the political life of the state as well. And the WBA and the AOH were getting in his way.

It was in this atmosphere, in a volatile labor-management environment heavy with virulent anti-Irish prejudice, that both Gowen and Bannan of the *Miners Journal* with the concurrence of Packer and Parrish began a prolonged campaign to link acts of labor violence and sabotage with a secret Irish organization called the Molly Maguires, and to link the Molly Maguires with the AOH, and the AOH with the WBA.

The theme was: all Molly Maguires are members of the AOH; most members of the AOH are members of the WBA; therefore, the WBA is creating violence and sabotage. The Molly Maguires, the AOH and the WBA must be eliminated.

The ultimate goal of the mine owners was the destruction of both the AOH and the WBA because they believed that until they did this their companies would be at the mercy of these organizations. And they believed the best way to destroy them was to link them with a secret, violent terrorist organization.

They were partially successful. By 1877 they had destroyed the WBA and decimated the AOH, but these successes did not result in the goals they had hoped for. The recession of 1878 which had gripped the nation did more damage to their organizations than the AOH or the WBA had ever done, and all of their carefully laid plans became unravelled.

CHAPTER ONE

Skeletons in the Family Closet

I first heard about the murder of John P. Jones when I was a small boy back in Dungloe, County Donegal, in the early 1940s. I had heard my father tell a number of friends how Jones had been murdered in Pennsylvania with a pistol owned by Alec Campbell, my granduncle, and how my granduncle had died on the gallows for the murder, even though he had not pulled the trigger, nor had he been present when the murder had taken place.

I had sat quietly in the background listening to my father tell about how his uncle had loaned his pistol to two friends, not knowing that they were going to use it to kill a mining superintendent, and how my granduncle had gone to his death on the scaffold swearing to his innocence and asking God to be his witness.

One of the most dramatic elements of my father's story, and one which came near the end of the tale, as Alec was about to leave his cell and mount the gallows, was my father's description of how Alec had put his palm on the cell wall and swore his innocence, and how the imprint of the hand had remained on that wall for decades afterwards, in spite of all efforts to erase it.

My father told this story in a way that mesmerized his audience, and I never became tired of listening to this part of the story, mainly because I thought it so spooky.

Over the years I was to hear the Alec Campbell story many times -- we owned a hotel and there were always new customers who had not heard the story -- and each time I heard it I always had the same reaction: I was bewildered that a person could be executed for a crime that person did not commit, and fascinated by the brutal and frightening way that my granduncle had met his end.

As I look back on my childhood and remember the many times my father had told the Alec Campbell story, I sometimes speculate about why he told the story so often, and I concluded that he did so because the execution had been such a trauma for his father and his grandparents, and they too must have told the Alec Campbell story time after time -- making the same impression on my father that his storytelling had on me.

When I was growing up, I often wondered why my father had never told the Alec Campbell story in the presence of his uncle James, who had been in Pennsylvania when his brother Alec had been executed. James was in his 90s in the 1940s, and he had worked in the coal mines in Pennsylvania for years and had visited his brother for the last time on the evening before the execution. Yet I never heard him tell about his brother's death, and my father never talked to him about Alec either -- at least not in my presence -- and I concluded that James did not want to talk about Alec because the subject was too painful.

In later years, when I really became interested in the Alec Campbell story, I would regret that I had not questioned James at length about the whole Molly Maguire era and Alec Campbell's part in it. But the young rarely think about such ancient history, and by the time I did become interested, James Campbell had been dead for years.

My father's story about his uncle Alec also contained a great deal of background information on the events leading up to the execution, and I am going to relate his version of it now, because it was the version handed down by the Irish branch of the Campbell family. In the years ahead I would hear many more versions of this very same story.

According to my father, Alec Campbell and his brother James had gone out to Pennsylvania in the summer of 1868 and stayed initially with cousins who were living in Tamaqua. Alec and James found work in the mines, where work was plentiful, but the hours were long and the wages low.

The brothers adapted to their new environment in different ways. James was only 20 years old in 1868 and he had the reputation of being irresponsible, and he continued to be irresponsible in Tamaqua, spending his money as fast as he made it and occasionally getting into brawls with those who disagreed with him. Alec, on the other hand, was 35 years old, seemed to believe from the very beginning that there were opportunities available in the United States and he had made up his mind to take advantage of them.

Both began working in the mines as laborers, and Alec soon discovered that the most money being made in the mines was made by miners and when he became aware of that, he bought his way into a miner's job within six months of arriving from Ireland. After two years of long hours in the mines and a rigid savings program he had a down payment on the United States Hotel in Tamaqua -- a combination tavern and rooming house that catered to Irish mine workers.

In the three years that followed, Alec Campbell bought and sold several hotels, always trading up, and he also became a wholesale liquor distributor.

By 1874, he was not only a successful businessman, he was a leader in the Irish community and an officer in a number of Irish organizations, including the Ancient Order of Hibernians.

During this period there was a great deal of labor unrest in the coal mining areas as organized mine workers got into disputes with the owners of the mines over wages and other benefits, and strikes were frequent and acrimonious.

Most of the union hard-liners were Irish, and many of these were from West Donegal. Those that lived in the Tamaqua and Lansford areas liked to congregate in Alec Campbell's hotel, where they received hospitality and encouragement from Alec, who knew what it was like to work hard for low wages in the coal mines.

After a six-month strike in 1875, which destroyed the mine workers union and forced the mine workers to go back to work, the mining companies decided to get rid of union agitators for good, and part of the strategy to achieve this end was to refuse to hire any union activist who showed up for work after the strike. The result of this strategy was a backlash of sabotage and violence, which included the murder of mine superintendent John P. Jones, who lived near Alec Campbell and who had been accused of blacklisting union activists.

Alec Campbell had not been arrested for the killing immediately, and indeed many months had passed before he was arrested and accused of being an accessory to the murder. When he was arrested, Alec Campbell was accused of having provided the murder weapon and of being the mastermind behind the killing.

My father had always claimed that his uncle had given his gun to the two men accused of shooting Jones without knowing what the weapon was going to be used for. Guns were common in Pennsylvania during this period and were carried by most men, and little was thought of lending a gun to a friend.

My father believed that Alec had been wrongfully accused because the mine owners not only wanted to get rid of all union activists, but also to get rid of all those leaders in the Irish community who were sympathetic to them, and they did this by indicting and getting convicted scores of union activists and community leaders -- twenty of whom were hanged after being accused of a number of murders.

11

I had often wondered as I had heard my father tell this story how the mine owners had managed to get away with mass murder, and why the rest of the Irish living there had let them get away with it.

I was always very much aware, however, that my father's audience never seemed as upset as we were by this obvious injustice. Usually they listened politely, and always with interest, but after the story had been told there were no expressions of outrage, and indeed no questions at all. There was just a silence until someone changed the subject.

As I grew older I was to learn that the Irish have an ambiguous attitude towards violence committed in the name of trade unionism. One can be viewed as a national hero if the violence committed is presented as part of a political objective, but murder for any other reason is viewed as just plain murder, and the fact that Alec Campbell had been accused of a non-fashionable crime, regardless of his guilt or innocence, was a mark against him.

However, after his execution, Alec Campbell's wife had sent a large package over to his parents in Dungloe which included items of his clothing and a gold ring, and when word got around the village that Campbell had been executed, people flocked from all over the area to express sympathy for the grieving parents. The following day almost one thousand people attended a memorial mass in the Catholic church in Dungloe.

My father died in 1955 at the age of 85, when I was just twenty-one years old. There had been a considerable difference in our age: he had not married until he was 41, and my mother had been only twenty-one at the time. I was the youngest of their eight children -- the oldest, Brigid Mary, is 19 years older than I am. In the last few years of his life, he rarely talked about Alec and I had no reason for asking him questions. James Campbell, Alec's brother, died in 1948, and he took with him to his grave all he knew about Alec Campbell and his role in the Molly Maguires.

By this time all my older aunts and uncles were dead and the last links with Alec Campbell had been severed. His old home still stood on the Quay Road, Dungloe, however, and his parents were buried in the Catholic graveyard, along with the gold ring that had been owned by their son.

But few people except the very old knew who Alec Campbell was, and, when I -- the last of my family to leave Dungloe -- emigrated to the United States in 1957, there was no one left in Dungloe who had the details of the Alec Campbell story. Only out in Pennsylvania did his memory linger on.

CHAPTER TWO

Another Version of the Family Legend

My sister Rose and her husband James Stamper were already living in Bayonne, New Jersey, when I decided to emigrate, so it was an easy matter for me to move in with them until I became settled.

My brother Bernard was single at that time and he, too, was living with my sister, so we formed, for a time, a smaller edition of the Campbell family.

The coal mining areas of Pennsylvania were only a two-hour drive away, but they might have been at the other side of the moon as far as my family and I were concerned. My brother or sister had not gone out there, and neither had my uncle Barney or the cousins who were related to Alec Campbell and also living in New Jersey.

Part of the reason for this, of course, was the passage of time: 80 years had by then passed since the execution of Alec Campbell. Another reason, however, was the fact that there had been no contact in my memory between the Pennsylvania Campbells and the Campbells back in Ireland.

The passage of time, the lack of information, and really, the lack of interest by my relatives in the Alec Campbell story, insured that a search was not attempted for relatives in Pennsylvania, and it was only I who had an interest in this piece of family history, but even then it was not the type of interest that would have prompted me to head for Pennsylvania as soon as I arrived. In time, however, I would begin the search.

I had arrived in the United States without a high school diploma or any marketable skills of any kind, with the result that I had to accept factory jobs which paid $1.25 per hour.

But I had come from a family which valued a college education and many of the older members of my family had acquired college degrees and were working as professionals. This gave me an incentive to get a high school equivalency and then to enroll in Rutgers University Evening School. I selected English as a major because I was interested in writing.

Eventually, I got a job with the Port Authority of New York and New Jersey, which owns and operates airports, tunnels, bridges, two transportation centers, a railroad and the World Trade Center in New York, and when I received my degree from Rutgers I moved into a position I found rewarding: marketing the World Trade Center and all its facilities.

When I was attending Rutgers, one of my English professors was Dr. Eugene Flinn, who not only taught English but also wrote book and theater reviews for the *Jersey Journal*, a north Jersey daily newspaper. Gene got me involved in reviewing books and plays -- an activity I have continued to the present, but with a different newspaper. Now I am a columnist with the *Irish Echo*, a New York-based weekly newspaper with a national circulation.

The books and plays I reviewed for the *Jersey Journal* rarely had an Irish theme, but I enjoyed this activity immensely -- in spite of the fact that this part-time work in addition to full-time employment and night school twice a week gave me a hectic schedule.

I reviewed plays all over the metropolitan area, on Broadway and off-Broadway, in amateur theaters in the Hudson County area, and even as far afield as Columbia, at the Delaware Water Gap, on the border with Pennsylvania. Although I did not know it at the time, when I was at Columbia reviewing a play, I was less than an hour's drive from where Alec Campbell had been executed, and where he lay buried in a graveyard in Carbon County, Pennsylvania.

Years passed while I continued to review books and plays and it was not until the early '70s that I next focused on the Alec Campbell story, when I saw publicity about a new movie entitled "Lament for the Mollie Maguires." The movie starred Richard Harris and Sean Connery and I went to see it anticipating I was about to see the Alec Campbell story on the screen.

To say that "Lament for the Mollie Maguires" was a disappointment would be putting it mildly. I was not only disappointed in the movie itself, but bewildered by the fact that Alec Campbell was not even mentioned in the movie.

The plot of the movie was similar in many ways to the story I had heard back in Ireland, but with two important differences. One was the fact that James McParland, the Pinkerton detective played by Richard Harris, had not even been mentioned by my father; the second difference was that the plot had as its central figure an Ancient Order of Hibernian leader named Jack Kehoe, and my father had not mentioned him either.

The failure of my father to mention James McParland seemed very strange to me, because it was obvious that McParland, who had gone undercover under the name James McKenna to infiltrate the AOH, was the major personality of the Molly Maguire story, because it was his evidence which had sent the Mollie Maguires to the gallows. That my father had not mentioned Kehoe either seemed equally strange, because Kehoe was being described in the movie as the leader of the Molly Maguires.

I reviewed the movie for the *Irish Echo* but did not mention the Alec Campbell connection. I reviewed the movie objectively and pointed out the obvious flaws in the film -- that the movie producer had been trying to have his cake and eat it...namely that he portrayed the Molly Maguires as both heroes and villains; that they were violent but motivated; that McParland, the Pinkerton detective, had betrayed many who thought him a friend, but had been sorry for his actions. The movie was so busy being a movie that offended nobody that it wound up confusing everybody.

I had noticed in the credits that the movie was based on a book entitled *Lament for the Molly Maguires*, by an author named Arthur Lewis, so I decided to get a copy of this book to see if there was any mention of Alec Campbell in it.

I found a paperback edition of the book and I began to read it with the same anticipation that I had watched the opening scenes in the movie. I was in fact waiting for the appearance of Alec Campbell.

I was 63 pages into the book by the time Alec made his appearance, and when he did he was not portrayed as the innocent businessman my father had talked so much about back in Ireland. Alec Campbell made his appearance in Lawler's Saloon in Shenandoah, to look James McParland over to see if he were suitable to be admitted into the Molly Maguires as a new member. Here is how Lewis introduces Alec Campbell:

"Lawler's was filled with its usual crowd and in addition there were a few men whom McParland had never seen before. One of these was Alec Campbell, owner of the Columbia House at Tamaqua, where he was both bodymaster and division chief of the Molly Maguires and Kehoe's second in command.

"Campbell was born in Ireland...He took an important part in local and county politics...the influence he wielded among men...and the power to overawe the more timid among his countrymen, made him sought, petted and pampered by the political wire pullers...He was a cold, unscrupulous man and would go to any length to affect an object politically or otherwise. It was darkly hinted he had been guilty of crime before he came to this country.

"Campbell cared nothing for the innuendos uttered against him. Campbell is supposed to have been privy to at least ten murders and is a man of strong will."

Lament for the Molly Maguires told a very different story from the movie that was based on it. There was no ambiguity in the book: no questions about who wore the white hats, and who wore the black ones. And Alec Campbell was mentioned time and time again as one of the leaders of the Molly Maguires -- "A chieftain among chieftains" -- and the innocent victim of family legend became a cunning and ambitious man, who plotted the murder of others and was proud when these murders were carried out.

Lewis, a native of Pennsylvania, wastes no time in showing how he feels about the Molly Maguires by attacking them in the first two pages of the book.

"From 1850 until 1877 three entire Pennsylvania counties and large portions of two more, with a total population of more than a quarter of a million, were without effective law and order in the face of an increasingly savage onslaught against on-the-spot representatives of absentee London, Boston, New York and Philadelphia mine owners.

"During the thirteen years between 1862 and 1875, there were 142 unsolved homicides and 212 felonious assaults in Schuylkill County. Many of the victims were mine superintendents, foremen or colliery supervisors, who had incurred the wrath of a Molly or a friend of a Molly..."

"Hostilities between the Molly Maguires and the operators were not battles between capital and labor, although on one side there surely was capital and on the other side the working man..."

"While a long, continuing conflict between employer and employee raged, the Mollies remained outside of it; the aid these tough men might have contributed to labor's cause was dissipated in senseless crimes of revenge -- murder, arson, mayhem."

Arthur Lewis' assessment of the Molly Maguires and the men who were involved in it made unpleasant reading for one who had been looking for an explanation for his granduncle's execution. The amount of murders laid at the door of the Molly Maguires was staggering, and the accusation that Alec Campbell had been involved in at least ten of these was something that I found difficult to accept.

Having revealed the catastrophic state of affairs that existed in Pennsylvania in the early 1870s, Lewis then introduces us to the men that will eventually bring the Molly Maguires to justice.

The first of these is Franklin Gowen, an American of Anglo-Irish background, who formerly had been a district attorney for Schuylkill

County, but in later years, as president of the Philadelphia and Reading Coal and Iron Company, was to launch an all-out attack on the Molly Maguires. Gowen was an ambitious man, who not only wanted to rule the railroads and mines of Pennsylvania, but the unions as well, and he viewed the underground Molly Maguires as a threat to his supremacy.

From his experience as district attorney, Gowen believed that conventional police methods were ineffective against the Mollies, so he turned to a private organization with a great track record against outlaw gangs. That organization was the Pinkerton Detective Agency.

Enter Allan Pinkerton, nemesis of the Jesse James gang, the Reno brothers gang, and the Younger brothers. Proud, sanctimonious, shrewd and ruthless -- and also short of cash in 1874 -- Pinkerton listened to Gowen's tale of woe and agreed to combat the forces of evil once again -- for a fee.

The pair then engaged in lengthy discussions on the tactics to be used to combat the Molly Maguires. Pinkerton proposed, and Gowen agreed with him, that the best way to combat the organization would be to plant a Pinkerton agent within the Molly Maguires, thus getting advance intelligence on plans for violence, which in turn would either enable the Pinkertons to prevent the violence or catch the criminals in the act.

Gowen made it very clear that he was not just interested in hanging a few Mollies -- he wanted the total destruction of the entire organization. Pinkerton said he would work toward that goal.

Pinkerton then went on to tell Gowen that the agent selected for the mission had to be an Irish Catholic, as an agent from any other ethnic group could not possibly gain admission to the Molly Maguires. Pinkerton said it would require a very unusual man for this mission, but that he just happened to have such an agent on this staff -- an agent named James McParland, a native of County Armagh.

McParland had been a Pinkerton detective for three years before he was asked to take on the Molly Maguire case, and he accepted the offer immediately, even though he was being asked to inform on men of his own nationality and religion -- a high crime in the Irish hierarchy of mortal sins.

Pinkerton told McParland he would use an assumed name -- James McKenna -- and would have to put out a cover story to all his acquaintances that he was going off to London on a special assignment and would not be back for a long time. No one, except Pinkerton and Gowen, was to know he was in Pennsylvania on an undercover operation. His pay would be $12 per week plus expenses.

Pinkerton asked McParland if he had any problems about informing on his own people and he said he had none, because all he had heard about the Molly Maguires was bad and that he would consider it an honor to help get rid of them.

Lewis at times becomes lyrical in his description of the courage and imagination of James McParland as he sallied forth into the wilds of Pennsylvania and gradually blarneyed his way into the Molly Maguires and became a confidant of all of its leaders, including Alec Campbell.

And when James McParland came out from his deep cover and pointed an accusing finger at Campbell, Kehoe and scores of other Mollies, Lewis portrays him not only as a great detective, but a courageous public servant as well.

For me the romance had gone out of the Alec Campbell story by the time I had come to the end of the book. Campbell appeared to have been a mass murderer and there was not a single desirable trait in his character.

Campbell had definitely been a successful businessman who owned a hotel in Tamaqua and he appeared to have been a power in local politics. But he had used his position as president of the Tamaqua division of the Ancient Order of Hibernians -- or the Molly Maguires as Lewis describes the AOH -- to plot the killing of Morgan Powell, Benjamin Yost, and John P. Jones, and did so because these men had one way or another had either offended Campbell or offended one of his friends.

I could neither condone or excuse any one of these killings, and the only conclusion I could come to was that James McParland had been right -- these Mollies were very evil men indeed and someone had to put an end to their activities.

CHAPTER THREE

Questions About the Innocence of Alec Campbell

My initial reaction after reading the Lewis book was embarrassment that Alec Campbell was up my family tree, and I was also more than a little relieved that, unlike my father, I had not talked openly a great deal about Alec, before I had found out the truth about him.

Then, I began to wonder if my father had known the whole story and had presented a sanitized version just because he was unable to accept the enormity of Alec Campbell's crimes.

The silence of my granduncle James began to make sense to me now, and so did my father's failure to tell the Alec Campbell story in his presence.

And I began to speculate about James himself and wonder if he had been involved in any Molly Maguire murders. Had this quiet old man I had known in Dungloe been a killer as well? Had he been involved in the ten murders Lewis had attributed to Alec Campbell?

Emotionally, I backed off from the entire Alec Campbell story, and I erected a few defense mechanisms to protect my ego. I told myself that Alec Campbell's activities were not a reflection on me, and that I was not responsible for deeds done a century ago. I also decided that the Alec Campbell story should be put far back in the family closet and that I would not bring it out in the open again.

However, after the initial shock wore off, some questions about the Lewis book began to percolate and I found myself thinking about the Alec Campbell story once again.

The most important question I had was that Lewis had not provided Campbell with any motivation for doing what he did.

Lewis had described Campbell in terms that suggested to me that my granduncle had been like a Mafia godfather who controlled an organized band of killers and who ordered all of the murders himself.

But the Mafia analogy broke down because Campbell seemed to have nothing to gain by these killings, as there was no monetary reward involved and no increase in power as a result of the killings. Indeed, the murders hurt men like Campbell and Kehoe, who were involved in politics and who had everything to gain by having an excellent reputation.

19

Lewis had also suggested in this book that Alec Campbell and other tavern owners had encouraged mine workers to strike, because when they were not working they stayed around the taverns all day drinking.

But he contradicts himself in another part of the book when he writes that the mine workers were so poorly paid that they barely had enough money to live on, and, if they had little money when they were working, where would they get the money to drink when they were on strike?

As I thought about these questions, I decided to back off a little, because I realized that I was doing what my father must have done -- deny that his uncle had been guilty. I asked myself if I were going down the same road by denying the whole story because the whole story was unacceptable.

I succeeded in banishing the Alec Campbell story from my consciousness for several weeks, but then questions about James McParland began to percolate.

For instance, McParland knew in advance that an attempt was going to be made on the life of William Thomas, a Welshman who had frequent confrontations with the Irish, and yet he had not warned Thomas, because he said he was unable to send a message to his supervisor. Thomas survived the attack.

McParland said he knew in advance of a plan to kill Gomer James, another feisty Welshman, who quarrelled frequently with Irish mine workers, but he was unable to get a warning to James, and James was killed by a man named Hurley, who roomed with McParland.

McParland knew in advance about the plot to kill a mining official named Thomas Sanger, but he stayed around the rooming house all day and did not telegraph a warning and Sanger was killed, again by men friendly with McParland.

Finally, he said he knew in advance that John P. Jones was going to be murdered, but he stayed in his hotel in Tamaqua the night before the murder and did not send a warning. Jones was shot dead the following morning, and it was for this murder that Alec Campbell was hanged.

My problem with McParland's account of his actions was as follows: one can understand that a single failure to act might have been something McParland could not control, but it stretched credibility when it happened a second time. And when it happened a third...and then a fourth time, then some serious questions had to be asked about McParland's role in these murders.

Lewis did not pose these questions, and he did not indicate he thought

20

anything was wrong with the way the Pinkertons handled the assignment.

But I had questions, and while I certainly did not think these questions indicated Alec Campbell's innocence, they were loose ends that ensured that I was not going to abandon the Molly Maguire story so quickly.

CHAPTER FOUR

A Trip to Tamaqua in Search of Relatives

After I had finished reading *Lament for the Molly Maguires* I had told other members of my family about the description of Alec Campbell I had read in the book and they were as shocked as I was that he had been accused of so many murders.

They were also surprised at the discrepancy between this version of the story and the version of his story we had heard back in Donegal.

There was one ironic sidebar to the whole *Lament for the Molly Maguires* story and that was in the casting for the movie version of the tale. The irony was that Sean Connery, who played Kehoe, was a childhood friend of my brother-in-law Jimmy Stamper and Richard Harris, who played McParland, is a cousin of another brother-in-law, Jerome Boyce.

Alec Campbell may not have appeared in the movie, but there was a Campbell family relationship there, nevertheless, even though it was indirect and far removed.

I thought little about the Alec Campbell story in the next 12 months or the questions posed by the Lewis book. Then, in my office at the World Trade Center one day the phone rang and a voice asked me if this was Columbia House, and for a moment I was startled, as Columbia House -- according to Lewis -- was the name of the hotel Alec Campbell owned in Tamaqua.

I thought at first someone was playing a prank -- a relative perhaps -- but then I discovered the caller was trying to get in touch with Columbia House Records, and the number for Columbia House Records was identical to my own except for the 800 toll-free prefix. The caller had neglected to dial 800 first, after he had seen an ad for Columbia House in the newspapers. During the next three weeks I got an average of 30 calls a day looking for Columbia House, and the result was that Alec Campbell kept coming to my attention once again.

This incident occurred in the summer of 1976 and when I told my wife, Eileen, about it she said we should take a trip down to Tamaqua on the weekend and try to find out if Alec Campbell's Columbia House was still in business. "We could even stay there for the night," she said.

That is just what we did...loaded the car up, and with our four-year-old son Padraic with us, we headed off for Tamaqua, which appeared to be about 150 miles away, judging from the Pennsylvania map I had acquired.

Tamaqua proved to be a substantial settlement spread out in a long line along a valley floor, with one major street, Broad Street, and a great many cross streets, as well as streets running parallel.

As soon as I arrived in town I checked the telephone directory, but did not find a listing for Columbia House, and then I stopped at several gas stations and made inquiries about the hotel, but to no avail.

I then tried another tack and produced an *Irish Echo* business card and told a number of perfect strangers that I was writing a story about the Molly Maguires and asked if they could steer me to someone who knew a great deal about them.

The first two people I talked to professed to know nothing about the Molly Maguires and the next person suggested I try the library. All three seemed guarded when I asked them questions and I had the distinct impression this was not a socially acceptable question in Tamaqua.

In the library, the librarian told me she did not know any descendants of the executed Mollies.

I asked a few more people on the street, but when I got a polite cold shoulder from two of them and no information from any of them, I realized I was going about the search in the wrong way.

I did not know how exactly I should be going about this search, but I knew that this particular approach was not going to work.

I had parked my car next to a row of neat town houses when I began to explore Tamaqua on foot and when I returned to it I discovered the car would not start. There was a woman standing at the door of one of these town houses watching my efforts to get the car going and, when she realized I needed help, she told me there was a gas station around the corner and someone from the station would probably be able to help me.

As I started off for the gas station, the woman introduced herself as a Mrs. McNeilus, and she invited Eileen and Padraic into her house until I returned. It was the first experience I had of what I was later to discover as the typical hospitality of the people in this part of the country and it provided a contrast to the wariness which had been the reaction earlier to my questions about the Molly Maguires.

I was back in less than 15 minutes with a tow truck and a mechanic and he took only five minutes to fix what had been a minor problem. And the charge was just $7.

Then I went into the McNeilus home, where I found Eileen and

Padraic dining on coffee and cookies and Mrs. McNeilus with the same guarded look on her face that I had seen on other people earlier. Eileen had been telling her about Alec Campbell.

Mrs. McNeilus told me she was of German extraction, but that her husband was of Irish background and that he probably knew something about the Molly Maguires, although she had never heard him talk about them. She said she did not know anything about Alec Campbell or the Columbia House and had never heard anyone talk about Campbell or his hotel.

Mrs. McNeilus was polite and hospitable but a little uncomfortable and we left soon afterwards, thanking her for all she had done for us.

A year later, over in Lansford, six miles away, I would meet another Mrs. McNeilus, also of German extraction, who was married to the grandson of Alec Campbell, and she knew all about my visit to Tamaqua the year before and how I had spent some time with the Tamaqua Mrs. McNeilus. She told me her husband and the McNeilus family in Tamaqua were related.

As I drove away from the McNeilus house in Tamaqua that day I thought it strange that a century ago the name Alec Campbell had, according to *Lament for the Molly Maguires*, dominated the news in this town, and now no one seemed to know a thing about him. Even great notoriety, it seemed, can easily get lost in the passing of time.

I did not see any point in hanging around Tamaqua, asking questions that would not only embarrass myself but others as well, so I turned around and headed for New Jersey, bringing back with me not a single new item of information on Alec Campbell.

But as I left Tamaqua, I decided I would make an attempt to find out what had become of Alec Campbell's wife and if the couple had any children. I thought it would be a very interesting hobby to see just what I could find out about the aftermath of the execution, and this decision presented a challenge which I found exciting.

CHAPTER FIVE

A Family Reunion

If I had known as much back in 1976 about tracking down people as I do now, I would have found the descendants of Alec Campbell with a great deal of ease. But as a detective I was a rank amateur at this stage and I spent almost a year in a fruitless exchange of correspondence with officials in Carbon and Schuylkill counties and with librarians in the area and not one of these people could tell me where Alec Campbell was buried or if any descendants existed.

I made no progress at all until the summer of 1977, when I was once again browsing through the pages of *Lament for the Molly Maguires* and I noticed that Lewis frequently referred to Molly Maguire stories printed in the *New York Herald* in the 1870s, and so I decided to use the same source as Lewis had used for his information. After a search of local libraries, I found that the New York Public Library had the *Herald* on microfiche for the period I was interested in and here I found leads that gave new life to my investigation.

The *Herald* had indeed covered the Molly Maguire era, both the trials of the accused men in 1876 and 1877, and the executions in 1877 and 1878. There was extensive coverage of the executions that took place on June 21, 1877, when Alec Campbell and nine other men were executed on the same day, four, including Campbell, at Mauch Chunk in Carbon County, and six others at Pottsville, in Schuylkill County.

The *New York Herald* description of the hangings was hair-raising, not only because of a total lack of sympathy for the condemned men and their relatives, but for the outright bias of the stories. I was shocked to read the total contempt expressed for the Irish as a people.

The trials had been accompanied by the same type of biased coverage, with the guilt of Campbell and the others taken for granted, and the most incredible amount of venom heaped on the Irish -- even those who were not accused of anything.

When the executions had been carried out, the *Herald* congratulated the sheriffs of Carbon and Schuylkill counties for dispatching the Molly Maguires quickly and with expertise. They did a good clean job, wrote the *Herald* reporter.

In the June 25, 1877, edition of the *Herald* there were several paragraphs on the funeral of Alec Campbell, which the *Herald* stated had taken place on June 24 at 10 a.m. at St. Joseph's church, Summit Hill. Alec Campbell's wife, a brother, two sisters, and a young daughter had been present at the funeral, which was also attended by a "large crowd" of Irish. The item also said that Campbell had owned a bar and a hotel at Storm Hill, which was near Summit Hill, Carbon County.

The information on the location of Campbell's hotel was in conflict with the information included in *Lament for the Molly Maguires*, and I wondered which writer had his information wrong: the *Herald* reporter or Arthur Lewis. I thought at the time it was probably the New York-based *Herald* reporter; I was to discover later it was Lewis.

The presence of a young daughter at the funeral immediately raised the possibility of Alec Campbell descendants being out there in Pennsylvania, and I was determined to find out if in fact they existed. However, the presence of two sisters at the funeral amazed me, because I had not heard of Alec Campbell's having had two sisters out there with him. I knew his brother James had been there, and a brother is mentioned, but the mention of the sisters took me by surprise and finding out more about these grand-aunts also went on my list of things to do.

My wife Eileen and my son Padraic were going to Ireland for the whole summer that year, and I decided to go out to Summit Hill and find St. Joseph's church when they were gone. I could not find Storm Hill on the Pennsylvania map, but I had no doubt I would find it, and perhaps then I would locate Columbia House, Alec Campbell's hotel.

When I was dropping off Eileen and Padraic at the Pan Am terminal at Kennedy airport for their flight to Shannon another of those peculiar little incidents occurred which were to happen time and time again as I investigated the Alec Campbell story.

These incidents were unusual...like all the calls I received for Columbia House in my office in New York, and the fact that my car broke down outside the only house in Tamaqua that had an Alec Campbell connection. I thought it spooky when they happened, but I have no other explanation for them other than coincidence.

Anyway, back to Kennedy airport and the Pan Am terminal. Eileen, Padraic and I were sitting in the lounge waiting for the flight to Shannon to be called when an announcement came over the loudspeaker asking that "James McParland who has just arrived on the flight from Denver...please report to the information desk."

Eileen and I looked at one another in amazement, because we both knew that James McParland, the Pinkerton detective, had gone to Denver to live after the Molly Maguire era and here was his name and that city being announced on the loudspeaker.

"Go up to the information desk and see if you can meet him," Eileen said. "Maybe he is a relative of your McParland."

But I said no -- he could not be. The Lewis book had stated that McParland had not married and that he had no other family in the United States.

"Do you want me to make a fool of myself by approaching a total stranger just because of his name?" I asked.

"And anyway, even if he were the grandson or great grandson of James McParland, what would I say to him? Would I say, 'Hi, I am a grandnephew of one of the men your grandfather sent to the gallows. How are you?'"

So, of course, I did not approach the man, and the man, whoever he was, did not know that there were people in the terminal thinking of him in a very unusual context.

The Saturday after Eileen and Padraic left for Ireland, I headed off for Pennsylvania again, this time to Summit Hill, which is located in the mountains above Mauch Chunk. Mauch Chunk had a name change in the twentieth century and is now known as Jim Thorpe.

Summit Hill is a small town and I had no trouble finding St. Joseph's Church, which was located at the end of the town, at the top of a slope that swept down to the valley below.

I went to the rectory where I was introduced to a young red-haired priest with a friendly manner, who said his name was Father Jones. I told him who I was and asked him if he could tell me where the grave of Alec Campbell was, and if he knew if there were any of Campbell's relatives living in the area.

He told me there were indeed relatives -- that Campbell's house had remained in the family and was located on Ridge Street in Lansford, a mile down the hill. He said that that particular area of Lansford had been known at one time as Storm Hill, and that explained why the *New York Herald* had stated that Campbell's business was in Storm Hill.

Father Jones said that a grandson of Alec Campbell, a man named Edwin McNeilus, now lived in the house and he picked up the phone and talked to Mrs. McNeilus and told her an Irish relative of her husband was in town. I was invited down.

Before I left the church, however, Father Jones brought me out to the back of the church, where an expanse of beautiful green lawn flourished.

"This is the old graveyard," he said. "There were tombstones everywhere here. Alec Campbell and his wife are buried near that tree over there," he said pointing to a tree growing at the edge of the lawn.

"But the graveyard was too hard to maintain, and there was vandalism. The Alec Campbell tombstone was knocked down several times, and so were the tombstones of other executed Mollies who are buried here."

"Look," he said, "Come over here," as he walked towards the area where Campbell was buried. "See...there is garbage thrown on the grave site. We find garbage thrown here from time to time. So, one of my predecessors laid the tombstones down flat and covered everything with sod. But the vandalism continues."

I asked him who was doing this, and he said, "Kids -- some of them over forty."

I looked around the lawn and in a way was experiencing something of a letdown. I had been primed to expect a spooky old graveyard with weeping willows and dilapidated crypts, and instead found landscaped sod, like the carefully tended lawns of some of the homes nearby. Things were not quite as I had expected -- and indeed as I got into the Molly Maguire investigation I was to discover that this experience was typical: that things rarely turned out as expected.

I thanked Father Jones for his hospitality and as I prepared to leave I asked him what he thought of the Molly Maguire episode -- if he thought they were guilty as charged.

He smiled and said, "Oh, you know the Irish never did anything wrong. You know that."

I looked at him for a moment not knowing what to make of that answer, and then he continued with the following: "My father was Welsh and a Unitarian minister, my mother is Irish Catholic. I sort of hear both sides."

I did not pursue the matter and left him and headed off to meet the McNeilus family. I would be the first Irish-born Campbell to arrive on Ridge Street since the 1870s. As I drove away from St. Joseph's Church, I wondered if Father Jones was a relative of John P. Jones, the mining boss Alec Campbell was accused of murdering. This was a very small town and it was definitely a possibility.

I had no trouble finding the address on Ridge Street when I drove down, but the building was not quite what I had expected. The description of Alec Campbell in the *New York Herald* had portrayed him as a very successful businessman who had owned a hotel, a tavern and a liquor distributing business and based on this description I had been expecting a big imposing building. But this building I was looking at was just like a large two-family house. My own Victorian house in Jersey City was as big -- or maybe bigger.

Mr. and Mrs. Edwin McNeilus were waiting for me and made me feel at home right away. I could not resist asking them if this were the hotel and tavern Alec had owned and they said yes -- there were a dozen bedrooms on the second and third floors and the first floor had been the dining area. The tavern and liquor distributing business had been in the basement.

I wondered just how successful Alec Campbell had really been -- this was not the Waldorf Astoria or anything remotely close to it, and I filed a revised image of Columbia House away for future reference.

They told me Alec Campbell's daughter had married a man named McNeilus and had five sons and three daughters. The two oldest children, John and Alec, died at ages 12 and 2. Then there was Monsignor Frank McNeilus, a parish priest over in Schuylkill county, Joseph, and of course Edwin. A daughter, Rose, had married a man named Phil Jones, then there was Mary, whose descendants are Boyles, and the youngest, Annie, who married a man named Bradley.

Edwin McNeilus told me there were dozens of great-grandchildren of Alec Campbell living around Pennsylvania, and the numbers were growing every year. "In twenty-five years there will probably be a hundred descendants around," he said.

Edwin also told me about Alec's sisters -- the ones I did not know anything about.

"They were Sarah and Annie, and both had big families. Monsignor Joseph Meiers of Wilkes-Barre is a grandson of Sarah -- he is your second cousin -- and Monsignor McHugh of Pittston is a grandson of Annie. There must be a hundred descendants of Sarah and Annie -- all of them your cousins."

When he mentioned Monsignor Meiers the name rang a bell and I remembered learning as a teenager that an American priest named Meiers had visited us in Donegal around 1950.

But I had not met him and I had not been told he had any connection with the Alec Campbell side of the family and I had assumed he was related to us through my mother or my father's mother.

Edwin McNeilus had erroneous information about his relatives, and he told me that his son had gone over to Donegal searching for relatives a few years prior to our meeting but could not find any.

I asked him where his son had been looking and he said it was in a town called Glenties, because his mother had told him this was the town where Alec was born.

I told him he had the wrong town -- that Alec Campbell had been born in Dungloe -- 15 miles from Glenties.

Edwin told me his sister Rose had also gone to Ireland, but she too had been unable to find the old homestead.

I told him that he, too, had an immense number of cousins in Ireland, Scotland and New Jersey -- and that they were also unaware of the Alec, Sarah and Annie branch of the family. All contact seemed to have been lost for most of the Campbell cousins, except for the visit of Rev. Meiers, who not only found the right town, but found my father's home.

I told them about my visit to Tamaqua the year before and they said they had heard that a grandnephew of Alec Campbell's had been asking questions, but by the time they had heard about it I had left and they did not know how to get in touch with me.

Edwin said people in this area did not talk openly about the Molly Maguires and would rarely talk frankly to strangers about the subject. He said his own mother had not been told about how her father had died until she was almost an adult and even then she was told very little.

"My mother never told me very much except to say that he was innocent...that all he did was to operate the tavern...and that he was never involved in murder."

"But she did say that her mother had hated James McParland and had called him a murderer. She had also said that McParland, Allan Pinkerton and Franklin Gowen were part of a conspiracy, but she never gave any details about this conspiracy."

We were sitting around a big kitchen table talking, and Edwin said that James McParland often ate in this room, when he stayed with Alec Campbell.

"He would drink in the bar downstairs and then my mother said that he would come up here to have his meals. Alec and his wife had been very good to him and treated him well. Then, he told the worst lies about Alec and got him hung."

Edwin wondered what kind of death McParland got, and I told him I had heard he had died in bed, forty-two years after Alec's execution.

"Well, maybe he got what was coming to him in the next world," Edwin said.

Edwin gave me a tour of the house -- showing me the bedrooms upstairs first. Then he took me down to the basement where the tavern had been and where, according to Arthur Lewis, all those murders had been planned. It was a big spacious room, that was used as a basement now for storage purposes.

I asked Edwin what his neighbors thought of the Alec Campbell story. "The Irish living around here believe he was innocent; the Welsh and Germans think he was guilty."

"You know, most people on the street think this house is haunted. Some small kids do not like to walk by the house after dark. They cross the street. Our neighbors claim they hear moans and groans coming from this basement all of the time."

I looked around the basement and it did not appear to be very spooky to me. I asked Edwin who the neighbors think is doing all the moaning and groaning, and he said the Welsh and German neighbors think it is the ghosts of the victims of Alec Campbell...the Irish believe it is the ghost of Alec Campbell who will not rest until his name is cleared.

"We have never seen or heard any ghosts in this house, but we know people who will not even come in here because they think bodies are buried in the basement. I am going to put in a new sewer pipe in the basement shortly, and I have to dig a trench down here, and I certainly hope I do not find any skeletons, because if I do I will definitely know my grandfather was guilty."

I was more than a little amazed that the Alec Campbell legend was very much alive on Ridge Street in Lansford, although the legend had different versions depending on whom you were talking to.

"You know, the people around here have long memories. When my brother Frank came out of the seminary he was assigned to a parish that had a German-American housekeeper. She was very good to him and spoiled him, until she found out he was a grandson of Alec Campbell and then she never talked to him again. She thought it disgraceful that a grandson of a murderer would be allowed to be a priest. This was sixty years after the execution. And recently the great grandson of another Mollie, who was running for public office, was attacked by his opponent as the great-grandson of a murderer, and he lost the election."

Mrs. Alec Campbell had lived for twenty-five years after her husband had been hanged and life had been very very tough for her. She remained bitter against McParland, Gowen and the Pinkertons until the end of her days and she always claimed they had murdered her husband.

The McNeilus family could not offer me an explanation why Alec Campbell would have been involved in murder, because they said he had nothing to gain and everything to lose.

"It does not make sense," Edwin said, "and that is why I think he was innocent. But what McParland did makes no sense either, and I really can't imagine why Gowen and Pinkerton would want my grandfather dead. I know he helped Gowen's political opponents get elected and Gowen disliked him. But to go to all that length to kill him makes no sense either. I really do not know what to think."

I left the McNeilus family later that day and I found the visit very interesting. The stories Edwin had told me were dramatic and when I arrived back in New Jersey I lost no time in telling my brother and sister about all I had learned out in Pennsylvania.

The visit also resulted in a renewal of my interest in the Alec Campbell story and I decided I was going to read as much as I could about the Molly Maguires.

CHAPTER SIX

Five More Books on the Molly Maguires

There had not been a bibliography printed in *Lament for the Molly Maguires* and there had been reference to only one other book -- the Allan Pinkerton book entitled *The Molly Maguires and the Detectives*, published in 1877. I had assumed this book was long out of print and that no other books existed, and you can imagine my surprise, therefore, when I went to the public library in Jersey City and found five other books on the subject. These books were *The Molly Maguires*, by Anthony Bimba; Pinkerton's *The Molly Maguires and the Detectives*; *The Molly Maguire Riots*, by Walter Coleman; George Korson's *Minstrels of the Mine Patch*; and *The Molly Maguires* by Wayne Broehl.

The presence of all these books sitting on a library shelf only blocks away from my home -- books which I had been completely unaware of -- taught me a valuable lesson about research, which I would find useful in the years ahead. The lesson was that I should never base any assumptions on what I read in any given source, because if the source was in error, then my assumptions were incorrect.

I had assumed because of the absence of a bibliography in *Lament for the Molly Maguires* and the lack of reference to other books, that the Lewis book was the only book on the subject around. I was wrong, because there were a great many of them around -- more than the five sitting on the shelf of the Jersey City library. And all of them had a tale to tell about Alec Campbell and the Molly Maguires.

I read the Pinkerton book first, and it was obvious that Arthur Lewis had leaned heavily on the book as a source for material for his own book. Indeed, the description of Alec Campbell's personality is almost identical in both books. Pinkerton, however, had correctly identified the location of Alec Campbell's hotel.

The Pinkerton book was obviously designed as an advertisement for the Pinkerton Detective Agency, and as such painted a self-serving portrait of the merits of its detectives, especially McParland. It was also obvious that Pinkerton had deep-seated prejudices against Irish Catholics and his narrative is laced with bias -- which seemed a little bizarre to me seeing that James McParland was an Irish Catholic.

Anthony Bimba's *The Molly Maguires* painted an entirely different view of the Molly Maguire era, however, and it was a view that was in some ways similar to the one I had heard expressed back in Ireland.

Published in the 1930s, the Bimba book argues that all of the executed men were innocent labor leaders...that there had not been an organization in existence called the Molly Maguires and that the name had been invented by Pinkerton and Gowen...and that all the murders had been committed by James McParland and other Pinkertons in order to frame the labor leaders. According to Bimba, McParland was a renegade bounty hunter who had betrayed his own people for money.

George Korson's *Minstrels of the Mine Patch: Songs and Stories of the Anthracite Industry* was published in 1938 and had a section on the Molly Maguires, which included references to Alec Campbell.

In the part of the narrative dealing with the trial of Ed Kelly for the murder of John P. Jones, Korson makes the following reference to Alec Campbell.

"Testimony thus brought out caused the arrest and indictment of Alec Campbell, a saloon keeper at Storm Hill...since the stakes were high the commonwealth decided to play its trump card, which it had carefully concealed...Jim McKenna, darling of the Molly Maguires, at last put aside his mask and appeared in his true identity as James McParland, Pinkerton detective...when McParland completed his remarkable testimony, the conviction of Campbell seemed inevitable."

Korson then goes on to say how Campbell "vehemently protested" his innocence throughout his trial and incarceration.

"Several months later, when his appeals for a new trial had been denied by the higher courts, Campbell heard the sheriff read his death warrant. Then he rose to his full height -- he was a big, powerfully built man -- and declared: 'It's hard to die innocent, but I shall not be the first. God knows that I am innocent of any crime, and the people know it, and the Commonwealth knows it.'"

Korson goes on to describe how Campbell continued to deny his guilt right up to the moment when the sheriff came to bring him to the scaffold.

"As the sheriff approached him, Campbell said brokenly, but with evident deep sincerity -- 'I am innocent. I swear I was nowhere near the scene of the crime.'

"And then, as if to impress the sheriff with the truth of his protest, Campbell bent over, ground his right hand in the dust on the cell floor, and dragging his ball and chain after him, took a long stride towards the wall.

Then stretching himself to the full height, he smote the wall with his large hand. 'There is the proof of my words,' he said, 'that mark of mine will never be wiped out. There it will remain forever to shame the county that is hanging an innocent man.'

"They hanged Campbell that morning, but the imprint of his hand stood out from the wall like truth itself. In vain did the sheriff try to remove it. Succeeding sheriffs also failed. Campbell apparently was right."

Korson gets back to the handprint later in the narrative and stated that it was still defying all efforts to remove it in the 1930s. By then it had become a major tourist attraction.

I read the Korson account with a great deal of interest, since it was the same story my father had told so often back in Donegal.

I have mixed emotions about phenomena that have a supernatural flavor and I had always viewed the handprint on the wall tale with a great deal of skepticism. But it was very interesting to see that my father's tale was believed in by many others, and I decided that I would try and get into the Carbon County jail at some point and see if the handprint was still there.

But the Korson tale had also jogged my memory about another story I had read in a microfiche edition of the New York *Herald*. When I had been going through various editions of the *Herald* in the New York Public Library looking for information on Alec Campbell's family I had came across an exclusive interview given by Campbell to the *Herald* reporter on June 19, 1877 -- two days before the execution.

The reporter was obviously hostile to Campbell and all the other condemned men, but he had been moved by Campbell's protestations of innocence, and he wrote that he "almost believed" Campbell was innocent. And there was a quote from Campbell which had direct relationship to the hand-on-the-wall legend. The statement Campbell made to the reporter was that he "would prove his innocence in the final hour of his life."

The reporter asked him how he would do that, but Campbell refused to give any other details. "Wait and you will see," he said.

Korson in his account of the handprint legend makes no reference to the *Herald* interview, and one can only assume that he was not aware of it. Certainly, had he been aware of it, he would have included it as an indication of the validity of the legend, because what better proof to offer than a hostile reporter setting the stage prior to the execution?

But, I concede that it is at least an amazing coincidence that the *Herald* story carried this prediction by Campbell two days before his death, and the handprint has continued right up to the present time to suggest the innocence of Campbell, in the face of the passing of time.

Minstrels of the Mine Patch contains an abundance of songs and stories about the Mollies, many of them written by the Mollies, and all of them claiming the Mollies were victims of a conspiracy.

Korson had collected his material in the anthracite regions of Pennsylvania in the 1920s and 1930s and the tales reflect the Irish-American point of view of the executions. McParland, of course, emerges as a renegade and a murderer.

The next book I read was Coleman's *The Molly Maguire Riots*, which was published in 1936 and was an attempt to write an objective account of the Molly Maguire saga.

The Pinkerton, Bimba and Korson books could hardly be described as objective, as the Pinkerton book was no more than a company brochure, and the other two had strong pro-Molly Maguire themes. These books were interesting, but since I had decided to get solid facts about the Alec Campbell case in order to get some idea of what the truth was, I could not rely on the point of view expressed in any of these books, since all three authors seemed to be biased.

The Coleman book gives an overview of the development of the coal-mining industry in Pennsylvania and the relationship between the capitalist speculators like Franklin Gowen and the workers who mined the coal.

He points out that the mining of coal was a highly speculative investment and that the mine operators had to bring equipment into the wilderness, which was both risky and expensive. The mine operators also either had to build railroads to get the coal out, or pay heavy freight charges to other railroad companies, and smaller operators were often at the mercy of both the railroads and the mine workers.

Given the nature of the risks, mine owners tried to get as much money out of the mines as quickly as possible, in case a flood or fire destroyed the mine, or in case the vein of coal ran out.

The mine operators cut costs wherever they could and one of the principal areas in which they were able to cut costs consistently was in the wages paid to their workers.

"Few industries had greater opportunities for exploiting workmen, and in few industries was the treatment more bitterly resented," wrote Coleman.

On the question of violence in the coal fields he points out that there were more murders in the mining areas of Pennsylvania in 1922 than there were at the height of the "reign of terror" supposedly imposed on the mining areas by the Molly Maguires.

"There is no evidence that they (the Molly Maguires) held a monopoly on crime in their day, as similar conditions prevailed before and since. Coercion and violent mistreatment of mining officials was, in many respects, peculiar to the time..."

Coleman also points out that an examination of the crime statistics shows that there was relatively little violent crime in the mining areas between 1870 and 1874, and that the violence that erupted after that coincided with the arrival of McParland.

Coleman does not come out and blame McParland for the escalation of the violence -- he is merely rebutting Gowen's contention that the Pinkertons were called in because of the widespread violence in the area.

Coleman then focuses on the rapid succession of murders that took place in 1875 and he points out that all that is known about who was responsible for these murders stems from McParland's testimony in court.

"Writers who accept McParland's statements do so because he told his story well, and never contradicted himself in any important detail under cross examination...the testimony of the latter (McParland), it must be remembered, was corroborated in detail only by highly disreputable accomplices, who secured immunity for their own crimes by testifying."

On the question of Alec Campbell's guilt in the John P. Jones case, Coleman writes this:

"Campbell was a leader of the Ancient Order of Hibernians and a man of more education than the majority of his associates. Formerly proprietor of the Union Hotel in Tamaqua, in which he was succeeded by James Carroll, he opened another place of business in Storm Hill, married into a respected family in the town, and appeared to be prosperous. His saloon was said to be the rendezvous for disreputable characters, but in those days most saloons in the mining towns attracted their share of such persons.

"Campbell had worked in the mines himself on his arrival from Ireland, and thoroughly understood the miner's problems. As an intelligent and influential man in the neighborhood, the miners naturally came to him for advice..."

"James McParland, as chief witness for the Commonwealth, testified that Campbell had entertained Edward Kelly and Michael Doyle at his saloon on the night before they were alleged to have killed Jones...that the

37

defendant was a leader in the Ancient Order of Hibernians, and that he had received Kelly and Doyle on their visit to Storm Hill were doubtless sufficient to convict him."

Coleman goes into the Campbell case in some detail and he examines the evidence and critiques the verdict. He makes the following observations in summarizing the case:

"Campbell's conviction was one of those which gave rise to the assertion that Gowen and his associates were using mere membership in the Ancient Order of Hibernians as a pretext of ridding the community of dangerous labor leaders. The nature of the evidence used against him made a defense almost impossible, as his counsel admitted. McParland had stated that Campbell had admitted complicity in the Jones murder. The defendant could do no more than deny having made such a statement, there was no way of disproving it...proof of his guilt, in the final analysis, rested entirely on the veracity of James McParland."

Coleman's final comment on Alec Campbell is a reference to the handprint on the wall of Campbell's cell in the Carbon County jail. According to Coleman, the handprint was still there in 1931, in spite of frequent attempts to erase it.

The fifth book I had checked out of the Jersey City Public Library was the Wayne Broehl book, *The Molly Maguires*, and, while this book was obviously based on a great deal of research, including Pinkerton and Reading Railroad files not available to other writers, it has major flaws.

Broehl attempts to be objective -- like Coleman -- but he consistently accepts the Pinkerton version of the story as the truth, and only disagrees with the Pinkertons when he catches them in a lie.

The approach he takes is as follows: he assumes the Pinkerton version is true unless the contrary is proved; he assumes the Irish defendants are guilty unless proof is offered of their innocence.

He has very little to say about Alec Campbell, but he makes James McParland seem like a heroic detective.

The Broehl book was published in 1966 and remains in print. It should be read with caution.

CHAPTER SEVEN

The Investigation of James McParland Begins

Up to this point I had read six books on the Molly Maguires, and had read a number of newspaper accounts in the *New York Herald*, and the sum total of all of this information was that there were two sets of stories being told about the Molly Maguires, one set portraying them as innocent victims, the other set portraying them as murderous thugs.

The portraits of Alec Campbell that had been presented were equally conflicting, and ranged all the way from innocent saloon keeper to martyred labor leader to mass murderer.

And having read all these conflicting accounts, what did I think? Well, confusion was the most prominent reaction, and I was confused because each writer had made a case for his point of view, and yet all versions could not be accurate.

Of course, the temptation was to accept the Coleman version, since it was well written...gave both sides of the story...made no attempt to defend the Molly Maguires...yet did not go easy on Gowen and the Pinkertons, or was unusually harsh on them either. And, there was that possibility offered -- that Alec Campbell was innocent. Of course, the handprint story was an added benefit.

Yet, I had problems in just accepting the Coleman version, because I kept entertaining the idea that, while there certainly was the possibility that Alec Campbell was innocent, there was also the possibility that he was guilty, and I could not accept either verson until I was certain one way or the other.

Coleman had stated that there was no way Campbell could prove his innocence and that in the final analysis it was Campbell's word against McParland's word -- and McParland's word had prevailed.

So, if I were to arrive at a conclusion about Alec Campbell's guilt or innocence, I decided it would be futile to try and prove Alec Campbell's innocence, but that I should instead try to determine if McParland had been telling the truth, and if I could prove him to be a liar, then I could argue that his evidence against Campbell did not constitute acceptable evidence of Campbell's guilt. And from that I could argue that Alec Campbell was not guilty of the charges leveled against him by McParland.

Having come to that conclusion, I decided I was not going to spend any more time focusing on what other writers thought about the guilt or innocence of Alec Campbell, but was instead going to focus all of my attention on the character of James McParland.

However, before I began to investigate the character of McParland, I realized I had to list a set of goals that I wanted to achieve, because if I did not know what I wanted to find out I would have a great deal of difficulty organizing this investigation.

When I gave this some thought, I decided that my goal should be to unearth information that would be unfavorable to McParland and of such a nature that had it been known at the time of Alec Campbell's trial it would have destroyed McParland's credibility.

The problem then was to define exactly what sort of information would have been so earth shaking as to destroy McParland's credibility. One possibility was to prove that McParland was a bounty hunter. McParland swore on the stand he was not being rewarded for his testimony and denied being a bounty hunter, and if I could prove McParland had received a huge sum of money for his testimony then this would certainly raise doubts about his credibility.

Another possibility that I found intriguing emerged from Wayne Broehl's description of how Clarence Darrow had destroyed McParland's credibility in another famous case out in Idaho in 1907, involving the murder of former Governor Stuenenberg.

Thirty years after the Molly Maguire case McParland had tried to destroy the leadership of the Western Federation of Miners (WFA) by implicating them in the murder of former governor Frank Stuenenberg of Idaho, but this time the miners had Clarence Darrow to defend them and he mauled McParland badly, and the union leaders were acquitted.

In describing McParland's downfall, Broehl described how McParland liked to quote the Bible, and Broehl also quotes Darrow ridiculing McParland as a hypocrite for quoting the Bible while he tried to send men to the gallows, and it was this item - this tendency of McParland to quote the Bible, which gave me the idea of yet another possible line of investigation.

Irish Catholics do not quote the Bible because the Bible is not taught in the same way in Catholic schools as it is taught in Protestant schools, and so Catholics do not usually make it a practice to quote the scriptures.

But Irish Protestants do quote the Bible, especially those from the north, and McParland was from the north, from Armagh, and his Bible-quoting raised the intriguing possibility that he had really been an Orange-man posing as a Catholic.

Suppose I could prove he had been an Orangeman who had accepted a bounty to give testimony against the old enemy -- the Catholic Irish? What would information like that do to destroy his credibility? I thought it would probably destroy his credibility completely, because the issue of McParland's nationality and religion was crucial to his success as a wit-ness. The reason McParland had been successful in convincing juries that he was telling the truth about the Mollie Maguires was that he made a point of telling these juries that he himself was an Irish Catholic who had gone up against the Mollies because he viewed them as a disgrace to the Irish people. Gowen and other prosecutors also made a point of emphasiz-ing McParland's nationality and religion and they characterized McPar-land as a religious man who was combating evil among his fellow countrymen.

I thought that the juries believed McParland because they did not believe that he would send so many people of his own nationality and his own religion to the gallows, if he really did not believe in their guilt.

So, checking into McParland's religious and ethnic background would be a goal I could pursue. And I believed that this goal, as well as the investigation into whether or not he had received a bounty, were two items I could pursue at my leisure.

Having decided on my goals, I then had to determine the means by which I was going to reach these goals. How was I going to determine if James McParland had a great deal of money back in 1876? How was I going to find out for certain about McParland's religion?

On the question of money, I had nothing to go on but McParland's sworn statement that he was only earning $12 a week at that time. On the question of religion, I again had only McParland's word for it, and the only person on record who had questioned this was Campbell's lawyer, Martin Lavelle.

My main problem with the investigation was that I had no idea how I should begin it. The Molly Maguire saga had ended 100 years before and all involved were dead.

As I began the investigation I knew from the various books that I had read that James McParland had been born in the Parish of Mullabrack, County Armagh, in 1844, and that he had died in a Denver hospital in 1919. That was all I knew about his vital statistics -- that and the fact the he had not married.

If I had been a professional detective like McParland, I probably would have known how to begin the investigation, but being an amateur it took me some time before I settled on a suitable strategy. This strategy was designed to accomplish my twin goals: get as much biographical information as possible; get as much information as possible about his assets.

Before I began to comb libraries and go farther afield in search of leads, I went over the five books once again to see if I had missed anything on the previous reading, when the main focus of my interest had been looking for information on Alec Campbell.

The only items I came up with were the fact that Pinkerton and Lewis had referred to the detective as "McParlan" while Bimba, Coleman, Korson and Broehl had a different spelling: "McParland." Broehl, however, noted that McParland had added a "d" at one point to his name and this explained the different spellings.

However, in some of the other newspaper clippings the detective was referred to as MacPharland, McFarland, McPartlan, McPartland, and McParlin.

The variety of these spellings disturbed me, because if I was going to start probing through old records, the first thing I should begin with was an accurate spelling of the name.

I began my investigation on several fronts. Given the fact that McParland had been born in 1844 in Mullabrack, County Armagh, one of my first actions was to write away to the Northern Ireland Government, asking how I would go about getting information on a person named McParlan or McParland, born in Armagh in 1844.

My next action was to send a letter to the Immigration Service in Washington requesting information on passenger lists of people arriving in New York in 1867. Lewis had noted in *Lament* that McParland had arrived in New York on September 8, 1867, on board the S.S. Valencia, which had left Queenstown, Ireland, on August 24. I included in my letter every possible variation of the name McParland, because I entertained the possibility that McParland may not have been his name.

After this I made a list of possible ways of learning more about McParland's later life, especially the date of his death. On top of this list was a will, which I hoped would tell me who he left his money to, and how much of it there was. Another item on the list was an obituary in a newspaper, which should also provide me with some personal information about the detective.

42

The existence of a will would in itself generate a number of lines of investigation. If I could discover who inherited McParland's assets, then I might be able to track down a descendant of that person and determine how much money McParland had when he died, and what McParland's religion really was.

Before I launched the search for a copy of McParland's will, I knew I had to find out the exact date of McParland's death and his last known address.

To help me with this project, I went back to the Jersey City library and got a copy of the Denver telephone directory and made a Xerox copy of all the listings for local government and state agencies in Denver. These included addresses for the Probate Courts, the Denver City Real Estate Department, the Taxation Division of the City of Denver, and a number of other agencies that might help me directly or indirectly get some information about McParland's assets.

Then, I found a reference book in the library that contained a listing of all the newspapers in the country, and from this I jotted down the names and addresses of these papers circulated in Denver.

When I got home I sent off a blitz of letters to a score of different organizations requesting information on James McParland, Pinkerton detective, born in Ireland 1844, died in Denver 1919. Address unknown to me.

Meanwhile, I received replies to my earlier letter to Washington, concerning the S.S. Valencia, and to my inquiry to Northern Ireland about information on James McParland.

The Northern Ireland official who wrote to me stated that there were no official records available for 1844, but suggested I check with the Catholic or Protestant Church the deceased had been associated with -- if I knew the name of the church. I did not.

The Washington letter stated that there was no record of any ship with the name S.S. Valencia for the year 1867, or any other year for that matter. Apparently, there was no such ship.

This was the second time in two years that I had been sent on a wild goose chase because of information printed in *Lament For The Molly Maguires*. Earlier I had searched Tamaqua, Pennsylvania, for Alec Campbell's Columbia House, only to find out a year later that it had been located in an entirely different town. Now, I had been chasing a non-existent ship.

However, this incident emphasized once again that I had to be very

43

careful about making assumptions based on secondary material. The possibility of error was always present.

The letters I had written to Denver were more productive, however, and within a short time I had photostatic copies of articles which appeared in the May 1919 issues of a number of Denver newspapers, noting the passing of Pinkerton detective James McParland.

All the stories were laudatory in tone, outlining his career in a favorable fashion, and making no mention whatsoever of the whirlwinds of controversy that had surrounded both the Molly Maguire case and the Idaho miners union case involving Clarence Darrow.

These obituaries also seemed at first to demolish one of my theories -- that McParland was not a Catholic -- because they stated that he had been a devout Catholic and a leading member of the Knights of Columbus, a major Catholic organization.

But after I thought about this for a time, I decided that if McParland had posed as a Catholic back in 1876, he would have been forced to carry on the deception all his life, because if he had not, then he would have betrayed himself.

In addition to this information, the obituaries also provided me with other important items of information: he had died in Mercy Hospital; he had lived at 1256 Columbine Street; his funeral services were held at the Cathedral of the Immaculate Conception; and he was buried at Mount Olivet Cemetery, Denver.

And these obituaries seemed to confirm that McParland had never married: all of the obituaries stated that McParland had no relatives in Denver.

Armed with an address and an exact date of death I sent a letter off with a check for $3 to the records section of the Probate Court in Denver, requesting a copy of the will of James McParland.

I did not have long to wait for a reply and the reply was disappointing: there was no record at all, from 1919 to 1977, that a will for McParland had been filed for probate in the state of Colorado.

I thought at first that McParland had died without making a will and that, therefore, there would be court proceedings either transferring his assets to the State of Colorado, or to the heirs that would have come forward to file a claim.

So, I wrote away again asking about the legal disposition of his assets: his house, his bank accounts, and any other assets he may have owned.

44

I had to wait two weeks before I received a reply that left me more astounded than ever: there was no public record in the State of Colorado of the disposal of McParland's assets. There was no record that assets had been transferred to either the state -- in the absence of heirs -- or to relatives or friends. I could not understand this.

I thought about the problem for some time and the only conclusion that I could come to was that McParland must have either disposed of his assets before he died, or the public records had been tampered with to insure that no dispositions of his assets would come to light.

The problem I saw with the idea of McParland disposing of his assets before he died was that he would have to know exactly when he was going to die in order to leave no trace of assets after his death. Otherwise he would dispose of his money and leave himself destitute.

Besides, if he had done this, some person or some organization had to have paid his final hospital bills. Somebody had to pay for the coffin and the funeral.

The question was who was that somebody and how to go about finding the identity of that person.

I thought about the issue of his estate for a week and then decided to get back to the problem after I had pursued some of the other leads I had acquired from the Denver newspapers.

I wrote a letter to Mount Olivet Cemetery and inquired about who had been maintaining McParland's grave, hoping that the person who was maintaining it would prove to be the beneficiary.

I wrote to Mercy Hospital and asked who had paid his hospital bills and who had been listed on their records as his next of kin.

I wrote to the Cathedral of the Immaculate Conception and asked if these records showed who had been listed as next of kin, when the dead detective had been brought in to the church for funeral services.

And, I wrote to "Owner," 1256 Columbine Street, asking if he knew how the property had been transferred from McParland's name, and who the owner was immediately after McParland's death.

I was hopeful that at least one of these letters would provide me with an item of information that would enable me to continue with my search for McParland's relatives.

I received answers to the first three letters, but no answer at all to the letter I had sent to "Owner," 1256 Columbine Street.

The Mount Olivet Cemetery regretted to inform me that it did not have a name on its records "concerning who was maintaining James

45

McParland's grave."

The Cathedral of the Immaculate Conception wrote that it did not keep such records and could not help me.

Mercy Hospital informed me its records did not go back that far.

I was back to square one.

But I had no intention of giving up as I had one last Denver card to play -- 1256 Columbine Street, which had been McParland's residence, and I intended to find out one way or another who had bought it from the McParland's estate and who that person had purchased it from.

A method of investigating this suggested itself within a week. I had decided to buy another house in Jersey City and my lawyer informed me that I would have to have a title search of the house to insure that the seller had clear title to the property. He said this search went all the way back to the original owner.

I told my lawyer about my problem in finding out information about the McParland house in Denver and I asked him what it would cost to launch a long-distance title search from New Jersey.

My lawyer told me I probably could get the information from the Denver Tax Department, that some city agencies were very cooperative and if I wrote to them I might get the information that I was after.

So I wrote away to Denver again, to the City Tax Department, politely asking if it had on record any change of title for 1256 Columbine Street, between the years 1919 and 1922. This time I did not wait with a great deal of confidence for the arrival of the information, as I had now come to the conclusion that checking out James McParland was going to be a very difficult task indeed.

But I was in for a surprise this time, as the Denver City Tax Department wrote me a letter which stated that 1256 Columbine Street had changed hands in May 1919, six months before McParland had died, and had changed hands again in May of 1920, six months after McParland had died. The person McParland had transferred the property to was a Mary H. McParland, and she had sold the property to a man named Casey six months after James McParland had died.

I was excited to find this link with the elusive detective and was feeling a little triumphant. I had not realized how much this search had meant to me until the letter came from the Denver City Tax Department and the name Mary H. McParland popped out of the page. Then I realized this was more than just a hobby I had become involved in and it was more than just playing detective. I realized I was totally committed to this pursuit of

46

James McParland -- although I did not know for sure why I was pursuing McParland with such tenacity.

Anyway, I knew there and then I was in this for the long haul -- that chasing the detective was going to become a mission, and that I would not stop until I had found out all there was to know about James McParland alias James McKenna -- the man who had sent my granduncle to the gallows. And I believed that this person Mary H. McParland was somehow going to help me run the detective to earth.

CHAPTER EIGHT

Who is Mary H. McParland?

Once I discovered the name Mary H. McParland, the first order of business was to find out who she was.

There were a number of possibilities. Since McParland had never married, this woman could have been a sister, a niece, or a sister-in-law. I ruled out mother and aunt because of McParland's age.

I read all the obituaries again just in case I had missed something, but all had stated the same thing: "James McParland had lived in Denver for 35 years, and he had no relatives living in Denver."

So, this Mary H. McParland, whoever she was, had been living in a place other than Denver. But where? New York? Chicago? Armagh? He must have been very close to her, however, if he gave her the house six months before he died.

The probability was, of course, that he had also transferred all his other assets to her name: his bank accounts, his stocks, his bonds, and any other property he had -- and this was the reason I could not find a will, or any record of the disposition of his estate.

Had the wily detective been thinking ahead -- that someone like me -- a Molly Maguire relative -- would try to discover his net worth through a search of the public records and had taken steps to insure that his private affairs remained private. It seemed a likely hypothesis.

The focus of my attention now shifted from James McParland to Mary H. McParland, and she assumed the role of primary importance in my ongoing investigation. Mary H. McParland had been the recipient of his assets, and therefore could provide me with information on his net worth. And she was almost certain to be a relative, and as such could enable me to investigate his religious background. James McParland would have taken steps to hide his original religious affiliation, but this Mary H. McParland, who had never been mentioned in all of the published material on the detective, may have found no need to hide hers.

So, I was determined to find out what had become of her, because if she had been a niece, for instance, she could have been young enough back in 1919 to be still around by the late 1970s, and, therefore, I had a chance of tracking her down and talking to her.

The problem was how to go about finding her. She was not mentioned in any of the obituaries, so, looking for her in contemporary newspapers would be a waste of time, as it was evident that her name had been deliberately kept out of the newspapers -- probably by the Pinkertons.

It was probable also that Mary H. McParland, whoever she was, would have preferred to remain anonymous. McParland had made a lot of enemies both in Pennsylvania and Colorado, and there was no guarantee even at that late date that some person, nursing an old grudge, would not take the vengeance on a next of kin that he would have been unable to inflict on the detective.

So, this Mary H. McParland had taken her money and faded quietly away, which was a very sensible thing to do.

The obvious need for anonymity, however, multiplied my problems in finding her, but I was not at all without hope of tracking her down.

I had begun to investigate James McParland when the trail was 100 years old, and eventually I had found a relative, and her trail was only 57 years old. It would be a tough assignment but not necessarily an impossible one.

At first, I toyed with the idea of going out to Denver and walking up and down Columbine Street, knocking on doors and asking if anyone knew anything about a Mary H. McParland, heir to James McParland, who had lived at 1256. But given the fact that over half a century had passed since James McParland's death, I thought this would not have made a great deal of sense.

Instead, I decided to focus on the period -- May 1919 - May 1920 -- which was the period when she had actual title to the house and see what I could find out about her during this time. After all, she would have paid real estate taxes and utilities during this period and perhaps the City of Denver or the companies who supplied utilities would have an address for her on file.

So, I went back to the Denver telephone directory once again and got a batch of new addresses for the various utility companies -- electric, water, and gas.

It seemed to me that since Mary H. McParland had been living out of town, she would have to have paid real estate taxes and utilities through the mail after James McParland died, and it was possible that there was an out-of-town address on file -- if the records went back that far.

I wrote letters to each of the organizations involved, knowing well I was on a fishing expedition, but hoping this fishing expedition would be

49

as successful as the one which turned up Mary H. McParland.

While I waited for the results of my latest barrage of letters to Denver, I continued to comb local libraries for any material that might be relevant to my continuing investigation of James McParland. During one of these forays I came upon a Sherlock Holmes mystery entitled *Valley of Fear*, which is based on the Molly Maguire story.

Wayne Broehl, in his book on the Molly Maguires, said that Arthur Conan Doyle had known Robert Pinkerton, Allan's son, well and had been a close friend of Pinkerton until he had published *Valley of Fear*, but that the friendship was destroyed because Robert Pinkerton had disliked the book so much.

I did not think that a Sherlock Holmes mystery would be very useful in my research, even if it was based on the Molly Maguire story, because I was after fact, not fiction, but I decided to read it anyway on the off-chance it would contain something interesting.

I read the novel and found one thing that would have made Robert Pinkerton nervous: the detective was portrayed as being very wealthy. But Conan Doyle had also made him a superhero and the Molly Maguires were portrayed as murderous scoundrels. It also painted a romantic portrait of McParland as he fell in love with a German-American girl and then fled the coal fields with her, two steps ahead of avenging Mollies.

Perhaps Pinkerton did not like the ending either -- the fact that the avenging Mollies eventually did catch up with McParland, decades after the Molly era and got even for what he had done to them. I thought it may have been that, but somehow my instinct told me that was not the only reason, and I went back and read the book a second time.

The second reading unearthed a paragraph I had overlooked before, in which McParland boasts that the railroad had the money to buy any witness it needed in order to convict the Mollies, and would do that if necessary, and I thought this was the item that had annoyed Pinkerton, because Gowen and the Pinkertons had always insisted that none of the witnesses against the Molly Maguires had been bribed.

But later on in my investigation I was to discover that there was one other problem area in *Valley of Fear* which was too close to the truth for Robert Pinkerton's comfort, but I did not recognize this area at the time. It was only when I was in possession of incriminating evidence against James McParland that it came into sharp focus why this novel, published in 1914, 38 years after the Molly era, made Robert Pinkerton so nervous.

Meanwhile, I received replies to the letters I had written to the Denver utilities company and the Denver Tax Department but they did not provide me with any useful information. Those that had a record of Mary H. McParland had only the 1256 Columbine Street address for her and no other address. This suggested she had stayed at the house until she had it sold. I had struck out.

In the ensuing months I went over a number of possible strategies that might result in another lead to this phantom woman, but nothing that I came up with provided me with any more leads. I seemed to be at a complete dead end.

CHAPTER NINE

Operation Armagh!

By this time the summer of 1979 had rolled around and my wife and I were on vacation in Ireland with our seven-year-old son Padraic. We were staying in Donegal with my wife's parents, and while we were there I decided to attempt to find out more about James McParland in his home parish of Mullabrack, County Armagh.

County Armagh is in Southeast Ulster and had long been a political hot spot, as confrontations had been taking place there between the Orange, the Green and the British for centuries. North Armagh is mostly Protestant and pro-British; South Armagh, which borders the Irish Republic, is mainly Catholic and is pro-IRA. The British army call it "Indian Country."

County Donegal, my birthplace and the birthplace of Alec Campbell, is in Northwest Ulster, and it is part of the Irish Republic. Ulster had been partitioned in 1922, with six counties, including Armagh, remaining under British rule, while three, including Donegal, became part of the newly created Irish Republic.

However, in spite of being cut off from the rest of Ulster, Donegal did at the time and still does consider itself a part of the province of Ulster and the nationalists of Donegal view the six other counties as being occupied by the British.

There was a great deal of trouble in Ulster in 1979, and Armagh was a flash point with violence erupting frequently. But I was determined to go in there anyway and find Mullabrack, because at this point this was the only lead I had on McParland and I was not about to abandon it, no matter what the political or military situation.

McParland had said on the witness stand that he had left Mullabrack in 1867, and while I did not in my heart expect to find out anything important after 112 years had passed, it was possible that someone in the area might know something about him. It certainly was worth a shot, especially since I had no other leads to follow on the other side of the Atlantic.

I arrived in Ireland in early July and I had been there a week when I decided it was time to go searching for James McParland's roots. A number of violent confrontations had taken place in South Armagh during that week, with four people killed, and because of this I was not exactly looking forward to my expedition.

I picked up a copy of an Ulster map and searched the Armagh area but could not find Mullabrack anywhere in Armagh. For a time I thought the name was another red herring dragged across his trail by McParland, but then I met a couple from Armagh who were on vacation in Donegal, and they told me that it was a parish near a village named Markethill, and that it existed even if it was not on the map. And they told me that as far as they knew that whole area was one hundred percent Protestant.

I was excited by this news, as it seemed to confirm my suspicions that McParland was an Orangeman, and I became more eager than ever to head off towards Markethill.

However, when I told my relatives about my plan, they said it was insane to be wandering across the border in a car with southern license plates and into an area where Catholics were not welcome -- especially those from the Irish Republic. The Irish Republic was being accused by Ulster Protestants of providing a safe haven for the IRA and the Protestants were bitter about this.

But in spite of the danger I had made up my mind I was not going to leave Ireland without going to Mullabrack. However, I thought perhaps I could do some preliminary investigation before I went in there, so as to minimize the amount of wandering around I would have to do once I got there.

I got a copy of the Northern Ireland telephone directory and scanned through it for McParlands and saw there were a great number of them in the North and quite a few of them in Armagh.

I toyed with the idea of calling the Armagh McParlands one after another, but instinct told me that this was not a good idea.

I suppose that my instinct was based on the knowledge that Ulster folk at this time did not talk to strangers, because a stranger could be a member of the IRA, a member of one of the Orange extremist groups, a detective, an undercover British agent, or an informer, and both Catholic and Protestant civilians were apprehensive of some or all of the above. And whatever chances I had about getting information in person, I had no chance at all of getting it over the telephone.

Nevertheless, I knew some advance investigation was a must, or else I would put myself in jeopardy by wandering the backroads of Armagh arousing suspicions with my questions. I really needed a contact, so I could negotiate this war zone with at least some degree of safety.

I thought at first about calling the British Army or the Royal Ulster Constabulary and telling them I was an Irish-American journalist who was doing research for a story involving the North, and asking for assistance in getting in and out of there in one piece.

Technically, of course, I would not be telling a lie: I was an Irish-American journalist and the story did involve the North.

But, the problem was that the *Irish Echo* had always been highly critical of British policies in Ireland and had labelled the Royal Ulster Constabulary fascists, and I myself had been one of the most vocal critics of the British among the writers, and there was a possibility my name was in some computer in the North -- ready to be accessed as soon as I made myself known. So, I thought it would not be a very good idea to ask the British or the loyalist police for help with my private project.

I thought of trying to make contact with the IRA and ask for their assistance, but I thought that would be equally unwise, since I was heading into the middle of Orange Armagh, and the IRA would hardly be able to protect themselves, never mind me.

The next possibility I thought of was making contact with clergymen in Markethill, which was adjacent to Mullabrack. I called the telephone operator up and asked if she had listings for churches in Markethill. She told me she had listings for a number of Protestant churches, but that the Catholics did not have a church in Markethill, and that there was just a listing for a Father Flanagan's private residence, which also doubled as a church.

I decided to begin with this Father Flanagan and called him up there and then. When he got on the phone he turned out to be a friendly helpful man who had more than a few surprises for me.

First of all, he had been in New York a number of times and had read the *Irish Echo* and knew all about the publication. He had also read my columns and was familiar with my views on the North.

After a few friendly exchanges, I got to the point of my call by asking him if he had ever heard of a Pinkerton detective named James McParland, who had been born in Mullabrack.

"Of course, I have heard of him," he said, "He done in the Molly Maguires. I know all about him -- his niece lives about six miles from here in the old McParland homestead. She is one of my parishioners. Her name is Mrs. Toner. She and her family are lovely people."

"Have the McParlands always been Catholic?" I asked, but I knew the answer before he told me.

"Of course. Mrs. Toner and her family are devout Catholics. The whole family has always been Catholic."

He must have sensed the disappointment in my long silence after he had told me this because he asked me why I thought the McParlands were not Catholic.

I told him that James McParland had been very fond of quoting the Bible, and that because of this I had entertained the possibility that he was a Protestant.

Father Flanagan said he thought that McParland's quoting of the Bible was very unusual for a Catholic, but nevertheless there was no doubt that the Pinkerton detective had been a Catholic. No doubt whatsoever.

This was bad news for me, of course. I had set two principal goals for my investigation. One was to prove James McParland was not a Catholic; the other was to prove he had been paid for his testimony against Alec Campbell. Now, one of these theories was being torpedoed by Father Flanagan. To say I was disappointed was putting it mildly.

I had told Father Flanagan initially that I was doing a story on James McParland, which was in fact true. But I did not tell him I was a grand-nephew of one of the executed Molly Maguires, nor did I get down into the details on why McParland's religion had been so important to me.

"Why don't you come on over to Markethill and talk to Mrs. Toner," Father Flanagan said. "Come to my house in Markethill and I will bring you out to the old McParland home. I am sure you will get some information from Mrs. Toner."

I was about to tell Father Flanagan that I was a grandnephew of one of the men that McParland had helped hang and that because of this Mrs. Toner might not be that happy to talk to me, but I decided that I would not tell him until I met him in person and I accepted his invitation to come to Markethill and meet McParland's relatives. I made an appointment to see him at 10 a.m. on July 13, the following Saturday morning, three days from then.

When I got off the phone, I had mixed feelings. My theory about McParland's religious affiliation had been blown sky high, but on the other hand I was going to pay a visit to the McParland homestead which Father Flanagan had told me had not changed in 150 years. And I was going to talk to McParland's elderly niece, who might be able to tell me who this Mary H. McParland was and how much she had inherited from James McParland.

The thought occurred to me that perhaps Mrs. Toner was Mary H. McParland, and it was she who had gone out to Denver to claim her inheritance when she was still single. Father Flanagan said she was in her late 70s, so she could have been anywhere from 17 years old to 20 when James McParland died in November 1919. I would soon find out.

CHAPTER TEN

Into The Lion's Den

My original plan was to make a day trip from Donegal to Markethill --
leaving early in the morning and coming back later that day. In order to
get to Markethill, I would drive 95 miles across Ulster, sometimes leaving
the main road to go on secondary roads. I thought it would probably take
me 2 1/2 to 3 hours to get there, and the same coming back.

But the day after I talked to Father Flanagan there were three ugly
incidents in the North, two of them in Armagh, near Markethill, and this
made me change my plans.

One of these incidents had occurred in Tyrone, near the border with
Donegal, and it involved the ambush of two IRA suspects by the British
army. The IRA men were killed and the British army, expecting retaliation, was checking all vehicles entering from the Irish Republic, and
since my initial journey would be through Tyrone, I could expect long
delays.

The other two incidents, both in Armagh, involved the murder of two
Catholics, apparently for no other reason than the fact that they were Catholics, and a violent retaliation by the IRA who killed four Protestants.

Given this volatile situation, I decided to approach Markethill from the
south, where I would be able to cross Ulster's southern border and I would
have to journey only 15 miles from the border to Markethill. Since the 15
miles could also be traveled on the main Dublin-to-Belfast highway, I
believed I could be in Markethill in 20 minutes after crossing the border
and would be reasonably safe since I was on Ulster's major highway.

But getting to this southern border crossing at Newry, by making a
long detour around the Six Counties through the Irish Republic, all of it on
secondary roads, could take more than four hours, so I decided to go to
Dublin on Friday with Eileen and Padraic and stay for the weekend with
my sister Brigid Mary, who lived in Dublin, and then drive the sixty miles
to the border the following morning. I could leave Dublin at 8 a.m. and be
in Markethill at 10 a.m.

My sister Brigid Mary took a dim view of my expedition into the
North, and hinted that she did not think too much of my continuing interest in the Molly Maguires either.

She pointed to the headlines on the *Evening Press*, an Irish daily newspaper, which told about two more Catholics being gunned down by Protestants at the Newry border crossing and asked if I thought it wise to be going there the following morning.

I told her I intended to stay on the main highway to Markethill and should be safe, since the people who were getting killed were being ambushed on back roads.

But she was not convinced and began to question me about what I hoped to achieve in Armagh.

"This niece of McParland's is not going to give you any unfavorable information about her uncle. Why would she? She will do nothing but praise him."

I told her she was probably right, but that Mrs. Toner might give me information without realizing its significance. After all, Mrs. Toner had no idea of the type of information I was after.

Then Brigid Mary raised an issue that I knew bothered her -- namely why I was bothering with this ancient story at all, because she could not see the point of it.

"Why are you so obsessed with this? It has been more than a hundred years. Why are you going to such trouble?"

I really had no answer for that one, because I did not know myself why I was being so obsessive about this story, or what I thought the point was. It certainly wasn't family honor, because I was drawing attention to a family tragedy few knew about -- or wanted to know about. And I wasn't sure I was trying to right an ancient wrong, although that may have been a part of it. The reason most acceptable to me was that the investigation was a challenge -- like climbing a mountain never climbed before -- and the reward was in acquiring information others had not been able to find. It was an off-beat hobby that only I understood and appreciated.

I was up early the following morning and resisted all further attempts by Brigid Mary to persuade me not to go. She even suggested I phone Mrs. Toner instead of visiting her personally, but I would have none of this and headed off towards the border.

The drive north towards Newry was uneventful, though I noticed that I seemed to be one of the few cars going north. I passed through the southern Irish towns of Dundalk and Drogheda and after that I saw a sign which read "Slow. Border one mile."

I slowed down and checked my mileage gauge, and when the gauge indicated I had traveled a mile, I kept an eye out for the Irish and British customs posts.

But I traveled another mile and no customs post, and then I saw a sign which indicated that Newry, Northern Ireland, was two miles ahead and I knew I was already in Northern Ireland, but I was confused about what had happened to the border guards.

I was to learn later on in the morning from Father Flanagan in Markethill that the customs posts at Newry had long been abandoned because the IRA had blown up the buildings every time one was constructed and as a result there was no border station in existence between the Six Counties and the Republic at that particular point at that time.

About a mile outside of Newry, the highway was blocked by the British army, which had pulled armored cars across the road and was stopping each car for inspection. British troops lined each side of the road, training machine guns on the occupants of each car that came in from the Republic, and all drivers had to submit to a search of their vehicles.

The machine guns looked menacing and the troops holding them looked unfriendly, and even though the people in the cars ahead did not seem concerned -- probably because they experienced this frequently -- I found the whole scene intimidating, and I began to wonder if I should have listened to my sister in Dublin and telephoned Mrs. Toner, instead of coming to see her personally.

But I had little trouble with the troops in spite of my apprehension. One asked me to get out of the car, and while I was out I was asked for my driver's license, an American one, which they immediately checked by calling my name in to headquarters over a mobile phone.

I wondered if my name was on a computer at headquarters as an "enemy" and I waited to see what would happen. Meanwhile, my car was searched thoroughly for guns, or bombs, or whatever, while other troops kept me covered with their guns. The troops were a motley lot: one was black, the other looked Indian or Pakistani, another looked like a Greek, and several of them had Scottish accents. The officer was English. The manner of all of them was cold and officious, but they did not harass me.

After a few minutes, having found nothing incriminating in my car or apparently nothing in the computer about me, I was handed back my license and waved on. I got into my car and was only too happy to take off towards Newry.

As I entered Newry, a sign indicated that the highway to Markethill was straight ahead so I kept looking for the entrance to the highway. But I had only gone a short distance when I saw another sign which indicated that the highway to Markethill was closed and arrows pointed to an alternate route. This route took me through the heart of Newry.

Newry, which has a Catholic majority, looked a little like Berlin in the aftermath of World War II. Gutted buildings lined the streets and shattered windows were boarded up. The town had been the scene of a number of confrontations between the British army and the Catholic population and the town had a multitude of scars that illustrated the intensity of the battle. On walls all over the town were IRA slogans, and the green, white and orange flag of the Irish Republic snapped in the breeze over numerous buildings.

Although it was only 9:30 a.m., the British army were all over the streets in force. I followed the signs for Markethill up a main thoroughfare and there were British soldiers hiding in every doorway with rifles pointed up the street in the direction I was going. I was the only driver on the street and I wondered what the troops were hiding from and if I was driving into the middle of an ambush.

I was very conscious of my southern Irish license plates, and I hoped that one of the troops did not get nervous and shoot first and ask questions afterwards.

But I was allowed to pass up the street without incident, without ever seeing what had caused the soldiers to take refuge in doorways, and within a few blocks I saw the turn-off for the Markethill road and I was out of the battle zone.

At this point, I had only been in Northern Ireland 15 minutes, but in that time I had gone from the quiet, laid-back Irish Republic into this tense, war-weary Irish province, where a very old battle was still being fought by the same two combatants: the native Irish and the British. The British had been gone from the Republic since 1922, and few inhabitants there in 1979 remember what it was like to have them around, but for the Catholics of Newry there had been no British evacuation and the war went on and on, much as it had been since the 12th century. James McParland had walked these streets as an Irish Catholic and knew the animosities towards the British and their Protestant Irish allies. There were secret rebel organizations here in McParland's day, with names like Fenians, Raparees and Molly Maguires, and these rebels fought the British and the Protestant landlords, much as the IRA was doing in the 20th century.

McParland would not have lived very long if he had become a loyal servant of the British or the Protestant landlords at home in Armagh -- they despised informers in this area and there was an open season on them, in both the 19th and the 20th centuries. If the Catholics were willing to take on British troops and British armored cars it is easy to imagine what they would be willing to do to informers.

When I left Newry and headed out the detour road to Markethill, I had only gone a few miles when I realized that I was on a back road that was taking me through the heart of Protestant Armagh, the very area I had wanted to avoid.

The change from rebel Irish Armagh to pro-British Armagh had come abruptly and without warning. I had only been driving ten minutes out of Newry, with its Irish flags and rebel slogans, when suddenly the British flag was flying from almost every house and red and white bunting was strung overhead across the road. I was in the middle of Orangeman's territory. I felt totally alienated -- and threatened.

I had been in the North often before. I had been to Derry and Strabane, both in West Ulster near the border with Donegal, and I had driven through Tyrone, when I was taking a trip from Donegal to Dublin. I had never felt out of place, or felt threatened there, simply because I knew that those areas are populated by a nationalist majority.

But here it was very different: the fierce display of British colors everywhere and the slogans on buildings which expressed animosity to the Pope and loyalty to the British Crown made me feel that I was in enemy territory and that I ran the risk of being ambushed by Protestant extremists at any time.

I knew, of course, that the display of flags had been part of the big Orangeman's celebration the day before -- on July 12th. July 12th is the major holiday in Northern Ireland and it commemorates the Battle of the Boyne in 1690 when the Catholic King James of England was defeated by Prince William of Orange, the Protestant champion, thereby insuring the followers of William of Orange a privileged place in Irish life.

The drive through the flag-decked countryside seemed endless, though it was probably little more than 15 minutes, and it passed without incident. I passed a few pedestrians, but if they noticed my southern license plates they paid no attention to them.

Suddenly, I was back out on the main Dublin-Belfast highway, and ahead of me was a sign that indicated that Markethill was four miles away.

I felt a little foolish for having been so spooked by the display of British flags -- which I had reacted to as being anti-Irish. But at the same time I was also aware that people were being shot dead in this very area simply because of their religion, so that some degree of apprehension had been justified.

Within a few moments I came to the turn-off for Markethill, and as I rounded a bend on the access road, I could even see it perched above me on a hill. I thought I had reached my destination with ease.

Then, my journey came to an abrupt halt as I was forced to a stop by a huge iron gate across the road that was padlocked shut. I stared at this barricade for a few moments not knowing what to make of it, and then I got out of the car and walked over to the gate and examined it.

The gate had been constructed of cast iron bars and was not that formidable a barrier, but it had a lock and chain and there was no way around it.

I looked around. The beautiful green countryside was empty of people and vehicles, and above me there did not appear to be any movement around the houses of Markethill -- except for the British flags fluttering in the breeze, one on every house.

The road on the other side of the gate ran straight up the hill to the town, so it was obvious that I was on the right road, but I could not understand why this barricade was there and why there was nobody around. It was like being in one of these end-of-the-world movies, in which all the population has been killed by some biological weapon and there is only one survivor.

For a few minutes I did not know what to do, but then I decided to turn around and go back down the highway to where I had seen another unmarked road that seemed to skirt Markethill.

I drove down this road and it eventually ran into what appeared to be another main road leading directly into Markethill. I drove down that road, but within a few minutes came to another padlocked barricade across the road. And again there was no one around.

I did not really know what to do next and I just sat there staring at the gate and wondering what this was all about.

However, within a few minutes a man came walking along the road from the direction of the town and when he came to where I was, he said, "You will have a long wait for that gate to open. It will be locked until eight o'clock tonight."

Then he went on to give me detailed instructions on how to get into Markethill, at a gate on the other side of the town.

"There is a gate there, too, but it is beside the police barracks and they will open it for you."

As he talked to me he looked me over, and he also seemed to be looking the inside of the car over very carefully. He seemed suspicious of me, and I thought he was probably a Protestant and he was suspicious of my southern license plates.

I did not ask him why the gates were locked, and he did not ask me what my business was in Markethill, and I thanked him for his help and headed off, per his instructions, for the entry point to Markethill. I found it without difficulty.

The entry point to Markethill also had a barricade across the road, and the police barracks that stood beside it had an eight-foot wall around it. But at the gate to the barracks there was a bell, and since there was no one around I rang the bell and waited to see what would happen.

The policeman who emerged looked me over carefully before he opened the gate and he also took a long look at my car and its license plates. He asked me what I wanted and when I told him I was there to see Father Flanagan he asked me if I was expected by the priest. I said yes.

He stared at me some more, and then I said, "You can call him if you like."

He stared a little while longer and then walked over to the padlock on the barricade and took a key from his pocket and opened it. Then he waved me on.

"The priest's house is at the top end of the town on the right side...if you don't know where it is."

Then he stared after me as I drove into Markethill.

Markethill has one long main street and it was all dressed up like the last outpost of the British Empire. Almost every house had a Union Jack flying, and bunting crossed the street from one end of the town to the other. Portraits of the royal family were in many windows, and the whole place looked like a stronghold for super-patriotic Brits.

While all this caught my attention, something else struck me immediately: the town was totally deserted, except for one very old man who sat on a stool outside a house.

I pulled up beside him, and he looked at my license plates and then at me. I asked him where Father Flanagan's home was, and he said, "It's four doors down. The one with the blue door."

He looked at the car and at me again and then he said, "Are you a Catholic?"

"Yes."

"So am I."

Then I saw that his house had no Union Jack on it, nor did it display any bunting. I pulled the car up to the curb, and the old man said, "If

63

you're a friend of the priest's you should know not to park there."

"Well, where will I park it?"

"He'll tell you."

I went to the front door of Father Flanagan's house with the old man in tow. The front door was open.

"Go right in. Ten o'clock mass is on. Go right in," the old man said.

I went right in and Father Flanagan was saying mass in a small room to the right of the front door. This was the Catholic church in Markethill -- a town obviously very Protestant and very British. There were four people attending mass: three women and one man. The arrival of the old man and myself added 50 percent to this tiny congregation.

As I knelt down and joined in the service, I could not help thinking that I had suddenly become an alien in my own country. Here in this part of Ireland, the overwhelming power of the Catholic church and traditional Irish culture had been reduced to a faint flicker of light personified in this priest and his tiny congregation. Had I been in Timbuctoo I would probably have felt no more out of place.

When the mass was over, Father Flanagan gave me a friendly greeting and invited me to have breakfast with him.

"We have plenty of time to go and see the Toners," he said.

I was full of questions. Why the barricades across the road? Why the eight-foot wall around the police station? Where was everybody?

Father Flanagan smiled when he heard my questions, and he answered all of them.

"I forgot about the barricades. I should have warned you. They always put them up on July 13th, because everybody goes off to the mock battle at Scarva."

Father Flanagan then went on to tell me that the Protestants won a great battle several hundred years ago and every year since they have celebrated their victory over the Catholics on July 13, with a mock battle at Scarva.

"But two years ago, when there was no barricades, the IRA drove stolen cars filled with explosives into the town when it was deserted, and when the bombs went off half of the roofs were blown off. Since then, the Protestant folk lock the town up while they go off to fight the battle of Scarva."

Father Flanagan's explanation cleared up the mystery of the barricades and the deserted streets, but I was still left with the impression that the situation in Markethill was more than a little bizarre. The fact that the residents of this town had to lock up the place so that they could go out into the countryside to celebrate an ancient victory was ironic to say the least. Somehow, the barricades across the road and the police barracks behind an eight foot-wall suggested defeat not victory.

But I had come to Markethill to get information about James McParland and not about this paranoid corner of Armagh and so, over breakfast, I got down to business and began to ask the priest about what he knew about James McParland.

Father Flanagan knew about the Molly Maguires and what McParland had done to them, and he had the main facts on the subject correct. But he had thought McParland had returned to Ireland after the Molly Maguire affair and had bought a huge estate in the south -- which was not true.

But, I recognized the story as probably having its roots in the Sherlock Holmes story which had McParland buy a huge estate in England -- which had not happened either, of course.

We chatted pleasantly about New York over breakfast and he asked me about my interest in McParland. I told him that I had had a longtime interest in the Molly Maguire story, but did not mention Alec Campbell.

After breakfast, he asked me to put my car in his backyard because the southern license plates would make anyone still left in the town nervous.

"They have nightmares all of the time here about cars from the Republic loaded with bombs."

Then we went off to see the McParland's niece in the old McParland homestead.

CHAPTER ELEVEN

In the Jackal's Den

The old McParland homestead was six miles north of Markethill and was the only Catholic farm in a prosperous Protestant farming community. The soil in the area was rich and those who owned farms in the area had valuable holdings.

I felt a little like an undercover agent as I drove up a country lane to the McParland homestead, which he had left more than 110 years before. Here was I a relative of a Molly Maguire using my status as a writer as cover, and I thought it ironic that I was going after the detective with some of the same techniques he himself had used when he posed as a Molly Maguire.

When I was introduced to Mrs. Toner, a woman in her late 70s who was also an invalid, I had a guilt attack because she, her husband and her son seemed so hospitable. And I felt twice as guilty at having got access to their living room by using the good will of this warm-hearted priest who was with me.

But my determination to find out all I could about James McParland enabled me to put my guilt to one side and to do what I had come to do: find out all I could about James McParland.

I told Mrs. Toner that I had been gathering information on James McParland in the United States and had talked to descendants of the Molly Maguires. I said I now wanted to find out all she knew about her uncle.

However, before I could direct questions at her about James McParland, she asked me what the descendants of the Mollies thought of him, and I told her that he was not exactly a folk hero in the coal regions.

Mrs. Toner said that was understandable, since the Irish do not like to forgive or forget. This made me squirm a little, since I was a living example of this.

But being an Irish Catholic and knowing I was an Irish Catholic she must have known in her heart that given the Irish Catholic attitude towards informers the odds were that I did not think her uncle was a folk hero either.

However, the objective of the interview was to determine if McParland had been wealthy, and if so how he had acquired his money. I also wanted to know who McParland's heir was -- this Mary H. McParland -- so I could try to locate her, if she was still alive.

I decided not to come right out and ask these questions, and instead asked her what she thought of her uncle.

"He was a very brave man," she said. "And a very good one too. He had to have a lot of courage to go down among those Molly Maguires, when he knew he could be killed at any minute. We were always proud of him here.

"I think it was his faith in God that sustained him. He was very religious and showed it later on in life by giving a lot of money to the church."

The mention of a lot of money immediately interested me, because she was touching on a subject that was central to my investigation.

"Did he give a great deal to the Church?"

"Yes, a lot."

"Well, do you have an estimate of the amount?"

"No, I don't. I just know it was a lot."

I thought it better not to pursue this for the moment, so I changed the subject.

"Do you know of a Mary H. McParland?"

"Mary H. McParland? Are you talking about his wife?"

"He was married? All the newspapers reported at the time of his death that he had no relatives in Denver. It was printed in several books that he never married."

"He married twice. His first wife died, and so did a twelve-year-old daughter. His second wife was the Mary you were talking about. They had no children. She wrote a letter after James died, but we never heard from her afterwards. She is dead long ago I am sure. She was the same age as him."

"Where did she write to you from?"

"I don't know. Denver, I suppose."

I wanted to ask her if McParland's widow had been wealthy but did not ask the question directly.

Instead, I asked what Mary McParland had done after her husband died -- if she had remained in Denver or gone elsewhere.

"I really don't know what she did. She was well off, very wealthy, and could have gone anywhere she wanted."

Since Mrs. Toner had said Mrs. McParland had only written once after her husband had died, I asked her how she knew Mrs. McParland was wealthy.

"My other uncles told us. The other uncles who went out to America. They told my father, and he told me.

"They were Frank, Edward and Charles. They all went to America and did well there. They never came back but they wrote often."

I asked her if they decided to go to the United States after James became famous, but she said they had gone out at the same time as him.

"They all left together from Belfast. They got the boat."

All of this was news to me. I had assumed McParland had been the only member of his family in America since his brothers had not been mentioned in any book, article or newspaper account. And on the witness stand in the Alec Campbell trial he had talked at length about his life in America prior to the Molly Maguire era without once mentioning his three brothers.

But the existence of these brothers, and the possibility that they had a number of descendants who might know a great deal about James McParland -- information that had not been published before -- opened up whole new areas of investigation and increased my chances of finding out a great deal more about the detective. First, however, I would have to find the relatives.

So, I asked Mrs. Toner to tell me all she knew about these three other uncles, as their lives and careers might have some bearing on the James McParland story.

"Well, I don't know that much but I will tell you what I do know.

"Charles was brought into the Pinkertons by James, but I do not think he stuck it out, I think he left them and went into business."

I asked her where Charles had gone into business, but she did not know. Nor did she know where he had lived.

"Frank owned a big hotel called the Hotel Cecil. James set him up in the business."

I perked up the minute I heard about James setting Frank up in the Hotel Cecil -- especially since she had said it was a big hotel. But I was also a little cautious, since Alex Campbell had been described in the media as a prosperous businessman who owned a hotel, and yet when I found this hotel, it was no bigger than a large two-family house. Perhaps, the Hotel Cecil was nothing more than a guest house with a fancy name.

I asked her a few questions about where the hotel was located...how big it was...how much it cost...and when it had been purchased...but she could not answer any of these questions.

Then I asked her what she knew about Edward McParland, and she told me she knew nothing at all about him -- except that he had created some kind of problem for his brothers. But she had no details on this.

I asked her a score of questions on the McParland brothers, but could get nothing more from her. She had no idea where they had lived or where they had died. She believed all had married, but she did not know if they had descendants alive.

Mrs. Toner's father had been Eneas McParland, who had died in 1938 at the age of 106, and she believed he had outlived all of his brothers. I asked her about the name Eneas, since it was an unusual one, and she said it had been a tradition in the McParland family to name the oldest son Eneas, and that tradition had gone back generations. She said another McParland name was Nathenal.

I had one other question for her and that was about James McParland's familiarity with the Bible. I told her how he quoted the Bible frequently -- a fact that had come out during the Clarence Darrow trial. Her answer was a simple one.

"There were not any Catholics living in this area when James was a boy -- except our family. The family always got on very well with our Protestant neighbors and when it came time for James to go to school he and his brothers went to the Protestant school, because there was no Catholic school, and at the Protestant school he was taught the Bible like the Protestant children. So he grew up like them, quoting the Bible. The Protestants were very good to him and treated him well and he was well liked by them. He liked them too."

I listed to her with a great deal of interest. She had given me an explanation why McParland had sounded like an Orangeman, and the reason was that he had been raised and educated among them.

This posed several other questions, however, which I dare not ask her -- namely, was a propensity for quoting the Bible the only thing he had picked up from his Orange environment? Did he also pick up their animosity to working-class Catholics, and did he acquire from them their poisonous attitude toward Irish rebels -- such as United Irishmen, Fenians, and the plague of Irish landlords: the Molly Maguires? Had he picked up everything except their religion? If this were so, it would have been very easy for him to turn on his fellow Irishmen in Pennsylvania, since he had never identified with them in the first place.

We talked a little about the United States and about the Ulster question. They seemed a little ambiguous about the Ulster question, and I got no clear impression where they stood. But they were nice people. I asked them if the family had ever been interviewed about James McParland before, and she said no. I said good-bye shortly after that and left without mentioning Alec Campbell. Again, instinct told me to remain silent.

However, as I drove away from the Toner house, I told Father Flanagan that my interest in the Molly Maguire story had its roots in my own family -- that my granduncle had been one of the executed men.

He said nothing for a time and then he asked me why I had not told him this in the first place.

"I was afraid they would not talk to me," I said.

"You're probably right there. But I would have liked to have known."

"Would you have introduced us if you had known?," I asked.

"I may have -- but I would have told them."

Father Flanagan had a right to be annoyed, and it seemed he was, and I couldn't blame him.

"These are very nice people, you know."

"I know."

"And you may very well come out with a lot of stuff that they are not going to like."

I looked at him and said: "Before we came out here, I asked you what the Catholics of this area think of McParland, and you said that no Irish Catholic likes an informer. I am an Irish Catholic and it was a given that I too would write stuff they would not like."

But he said I should have told him about the family connection, and I did not argue, since he had a point.

We parted company in Markethill, with a little tension in the air -- him a little annoyed; I feeling a little guilty.

It was an easy journey back to the border. For one thing, I had become used to all those British flags and did not pay any attention to them on the way back. My paranoia about Orange assassins had also vanished, and I even felt relaxed when I was stopped and searched by British troops in Newry. In one short day, I had gone from being alienated by the Ulster situation to accepting it, which shows that one can get used to anything.

When I arrived back in Dublin, Eileen and Brigid Mary were glad to see me and I told them all about my adventure.

CHAPTER TWELVE

The Investigation of Mrs. James McParland

When I arrived back in the United States I made a list of possible ways of continuing with my investigation. I put the Hotel Cecil at the top of the list and Mary H. McParland as number two. Charles and Edward McParland came next on my list.

Mrs. Toner had told me James had set up Frank in the Hotel Cecil, so my number one priority was to locate this hotel, find out when Frank McParland had purchased it, and find out how much he had paid for it. The amount of the payment would be the money James had given him.

My first approach to finding the Hotel Cecil was to go to the New York Public Library and see if there was a directory of hotels in existence for the 1880s that would list all the hotels in the United States. There was no such directory on file.

I was told at the library, however, that the best way to go about the search was to get street directory listings of various cities for the 19th century and also to get the histories of major cities and to check for a mention of the Hotel Cecil

I did just that: I wrote away to the public libraries in all major American cities and asked if they could provide me with Xerox copies of street directories for the 1880s, focusing on the page which might list the Hotel Cecil and over a six month period I got a reply from all of them but the Hotel Cecil was not in any of the directories.

I then tried 1890 - 1900, 1900 - 1910, 1910 - 1920, but again struck out.

Next, I acquired the history of every American city, and thumbed through the index for a mention of the Hotel Cecil, but again I could not find a mention of such an establishment.

The results suggested two possibilities: one, that there was no such establishment; two, that it had not been worth mentioning because it was too small.

I decided to put the Hotel Cecil on the back burner and turn my attention to Mary H. McParland once again.

By this time my slow-paced pursuit of James McParland had consumed a great deal of time and energy, with months turning into years and information coming very slowly. There were times when I would drop the investigation for six months at a time, but I would always go back to it and continue to follow leads.

By 1982, when I resumed my pursuit of Mary H. McParland, I had written hundreds of letters all over the country and received a mountain of correspondence in return, but progress was very slow.

At one point in 1982, I had purchased a city map of Denver and had noted all the street numbers on Columbine Street, and then wrote a letter to every house in the block on which McParland had lived, hoping to turn up someone who had known his wife, but I did not receive any information.

I wrote away to all the newspapers in Denver that had been around in the twenties and thirties, inquiring if any of them had ever carried an obituary on Mary H. McParland, but none of them had done so.

I wondered if the Pinkertons had persuaded the media not to mention the existence of Mary H. McParland, when they wrote McParland's obituary back in 1918. What other reason would there have been for failing to note that this famous Denver citizen had a wife. The fact that he was married must have been well known to the press at the time.

I wondered if the Pinkertons would still cover up the existence of Mary H. McParland, even after all this time, and this gave me the idea of testing out whether or not they would.

So I wrote a letter to the Pinkerton office in Denver asking for the names and addresses of the relatives of James McParland who had been living in Denver in 1918, when McParland had died. I stated in the letter that members of my family "had known" the detective -- which was of course true. I wrote the letter in a friendly manner and waited to see what would happen.

I got a polite letter back which informed me that the only relative that McParland had in Denver when he died was a sister-in-law named Mother Regis, who was head of the Mercy Hospital in Denver. No mention at all was made of a wife or brothers.

I thought this over for a while as I wondered who this Mother Superior was. She could have been Mary H. McParland's sister, or the widow of one of his brothers who had entered a convent.

In either case, thanks to the Pinkertons I had something to work on. I wondered, if the Pinkertons had known what I was up to, whether they would have been so cooperative.

My next letter went to the Mercy Hospital in Denver, asking for biographical information on Mother Regis. I was confident that I would get this information, since she had been the Mother Superior of the hospital, but I got a letter back that the hospital had nothing on file. I thought this was odd.

Then I wrote to the headquarters of the Mercy Sisters in Denver and asked for information on Mother Regis -- but with the same result. There was none on file.

It seemed like I had reached another dead end, and I wondered if James McParland was reaching out from the grave to checkmate every move I made. Every time I tried to find out information about his finances or his relatives I met with the same results.

As I thought of McParland in his grave another idea came to me, and afterwards I wondered why I had not thought of it before. Mrs. Toner over in Armagh had said that Mrs. James McParland must have been dead for decades, and if she were dead where else would she have been buried except with the husband. My quarry would be buried with McParland in the Mount Olivet Cemetery in Denver, and the cemetery should have her last known address.

So, I wrote a letter to the Mount Olivet Cemetery requesting the date of burial of Mary H. McParland, and also her last known address. I stated she was the wife of James McParland.

Within a week, a letter came back that stated that burial had taken place on November 22, 1928, but there was no address on file and the writer did not know where I might find it. Once again, I was facing obstacles in pursuing this elusive woman.

Next I sent a letter off with $3 to the Bureau of Vital Statistics which keeps track of births and deaths and requested a death certificate on Mary H. McParland. But within a week I got a letter back telling me that there was no record on file of the death of Mary H. McParland.

This left me with two possibilities: one, she did not die in the City of Denver; two, someone had removed the death record. I had no idea which was the more plausible.

I decided to turn my attention to Mother Regis again, unwilling to believe that I could not get information out of the Mercy Sisters about her. I would have written to the Bureau of Vital Statistics for her death certificate except I did not have her surname -- or her first name.

Then I had an idea that seemed to be a long shot but was worth a try. I wrote back to the Mercy Convent sending the same series of questions about Mother Regis I had sent before but this time asking that the letter be given to the oldest nun in the convent who might have been there in the 1920s.

I had to wait a month before I got a reply and when I did I got information that gave life to my investigation once again. My correspondent was an elderly nun who had known Mother Regis and also about her relationship with James McParland.

Sister Mary, who wrote to me, said Mother Regis was the sister of Mary H. McParland and that Mother Regis had died in 1926. She said that Mary H. McParland and two other sisters, a Mrs. Albert Tebo and Mrs. William Sammons, had come to the funeral in Denver, and that all three sisters had been living in Chicago at that time. The old nun regretted she had no Chicago address for Mary H. McParland.

As I read the letter I realized that my intuition about Mary H. McParland had been correct -- that she had moved out of Denver. I would have been wasting my time going to Denver to walk up and down Columbine Street looking for someone who knew her.

My investigation of Mary H. McParland would now switch to another city, where I would attempt to find out as much as I could about her.

CHAPTER THIRTEEN

Mrs. McParland and the Windy City

By this time I had become a little more skilled in investigating and I did not view the Chicago phase of investigation as a major undertaking.

I began to pursue Mary H. McParland in Chicago in the spring of 1983 and in spite of the fact that 55 years had passed since she died, I was confident of getting more information on her.

The first thing I did was to write away for a copy of her death certificate as this was the obvious way of getting her address, as I had learned from the Denver part of my investigation. I sent $3.00 off to the Cook Country Bureau of Vital Statistics with a letter stating her date of death.

I got a death certificate back within a week, but it was for a Mary McPartland, with an extra "t," and it was the death certificate of a 49-year-old who had died three months after Mary H. McParland. Also the death certificate listed the husband's name as Bernard, and the husband had still been alive when the wife died. I pointed out the error to the Bureau of Vital Statistics and within a week I had the correct certificate in my possession.

The death certificate gave me the address I was looking for: 711 Waveland Avenue, Chicago. It gave her age: 69; her place of birth: Princeton, Wisconsin; and the date of death as November 19, 1928. It also gave her maiden name -- Regan -- and her parents names and their place of birth: Ireland.

Suddenly, Mary H. McParland changed in my perception from a shadowy figure without substance into a real person, whose age I knew, whose maiden name I knew, and who had parents, and a home address.

She had been younger than McParland -- 16 years younger -- and she had been only 17 when Alec Campbell was hanged. I wondered how long she had been married to McParland, since she was his second wife. I also wondered if she had been living with him when he died, because if they had separated this might explain why the newspapers did not mention her when McParland died.

On the other hand, the failure to mention her may have been deliberate, a device to protect her from the enemies McParland had accumulated in his lifetime.

Finding out her age, her address and her date of death was just another step in my investigation -- I had now to determine what her assets were and to track these assets back to McParland and then back through him to the Molly Maguire era.

I had little illusions about the immensity of the project, and I also knew that persistence is not just enough in such research -- that luck also can play a major role. For instance, if the Pinkerton office in Denver had not let me know about Mother Regis, then I would not have located the elderly nun in the Mercy Convent, who in turn had told me where to look for Mary H. McParland. If that sequence of events had not occurred I might still be looking for Mary H. McParland in Denver.

The first step in the next phase of my investigation was to write to the Chicago Probate Court and inquire if a will for Mary H. McParland was on file. The court wrote back, indicating that such a document did exist, and that I could have a copy of it for $5. I sent the money immediately.

As I waited for the document to arrive I speculated on just how much she had in her possession when she died. I expected at least several hundred thousand dollars, since Mrs. Toner over in Armagh had said McParland had left his wife very well off when he died in 1918.

I realized, of course, that proof that Mrs. McParland was a wealthy widow was not proof that this wealth was the proceeds of a Molly Maguire bounty. I still would have to trace the money all the way back to the 1870s.

I did not have a strategy for tracing the widow's assets back in time, and I had decided to just wait and see what those assets were before I began to worry about the next step.

The Chicago Probate Court took about ten days to mail the documents I had sent away for and the large manila envelope that arrived in the mail was bulky and contained a score of legal-size documents.

I did not read these documents in the order they had been prepared, but instead thumbed quickly through them, looking for the one which summarized her total assets.

I found it easily -- and suffered a major disappointment. Mary H. McParland's total assets, according to these documents, had been just over $16,000, all of it in cash and in bonds.

This was far below the amount I had expected, even taking into consideration that every 1928 dollar was probably worth $6 in 1983. A sum of $100,000 in 1983 dollars is not a great deal of money when one considers she had sold a house in Denver and had been married to a sup-

76

posedly wealthy man.

I almost ended the investigation there and then because I was so disappointed at what the probated estate of Mary H. McParland had revealed. I had, of course, good reason for quitting the investigation. I had started off the investigation with two major goals: one, to prove that McParland was a Protestant; two, that he had a fortune that he had acquired from selling out the Molly Maguires. My journey to Armagh had blown the Orangeman theory sky high, and now these documents from Chicago had lit a fire under the second one.

As I thought about the demolition of my two theories I had to come face to face with the possibility that McParland had been everything he had said he was: a courageous detective who had brought a gang of terrorists to justice.

I went over all the documents that I had received and saw that Mary H. McParland had left her assets to her two sisters, Mrs. Tebo and Mrs. Sammons. Each received one half, with some $500 left for masses and a "small diamond ring left to a Catherine McParland."

Who was this Catherine McParland? Certainly nor James McParland's daughter by his first wife -- she had died at the age of twelve. A niece? A sister-in-law? A sister? No, it couldn't be a sister, as he did not have any.

The gift of one small piece of jewelry seemed like a token gift, like the gift one would give to a child, or a young person. Perhaps she was McParland's favorite niece -- the daughter of one of his brothers.

As I tried to decide on whether or not to abandon the investigation, I thought that this Catherine McParland could very well be still alive, and therefore I might be able to locate her and talk to her. Fifty-three years had passed since the time the will had been probated, but if she had been in her teens or in her twenties back in 1929, then she could be anywhere from 70 years old to 80 years old.

As I went through the documents I noted that while this person had been referred to as Catherine McParland in 1928 and 1929, that in the document which dealt with the final disposition of the assets, she was referred to as Catherine McParland Murphy. It would appear that she was a young woman who had recently married.

I then decided I should stay in there for a little while longer and try to locate this person. I had some loose ends still to tie up which had supported my original theory about McParland's wealth -- namely the issue of the Hotel Cecil, which James McParland had purchased for his brother

Frank. I did not want to end the investigation without at least locating it. I thought it possible James McParland had put all the Molly Maguire money into this establishment and then saw the hotel go bankrupt. It was possible.

Another issue was whether or not I should assume that Mary H. McParland was not that affluent because she did not leave a big estate. There was the possibility that she had used the same tactic that her husband had: transferring the bulk of her assets to someone before she died, keeping only what she needed for living expenses.

The more I thought of this the more I thought it worth while to continue the investigation until such time as I had no other possible leads to follow.

Instinctively I knew that if I abandoned the investigation at this point I would not be able to put it behind me and would return to it at some later point in time.

So, I decided to go on until I had settled the McParland case once and for all.

* * * *

I was to spend the next six months in a futile attempt to investigate Mary H. McParland's finances. More than 90% of her assets had been in stocks, with the bulk of the stock invested in the Mountain States Telegraph and Telephone Company, and the sequence numbers of these stocks suggested that these stocks had been part of a bigger block of stocks the McParlands had owned at one time, but had disposed of.

For instance, she had certificate #11026 for four shares of telephone stock, priced at $400; she had certificate #11036 for three shares -- $300; and certificate #11070 for one share -- $100. She had a number of other telephone company certificates, including #3187, which was valued at $2,500.

All of the above certificates were bought from the Denver-based company, presumably when the McParlands were living in Denver, and when I wrote to the company headquarters and asked for an accounting of any other certificates the McParlands may have owned when they were alive, I got a call from a telephone company executive who was very polite and very evasive, and very curious to find out why I wanted the information on James McParland.

During the conversation, I did not mention the Pinkerton connection,

78

or the Molly Maguire connection and neither did he. I wanted to know just how many of those certificates McParland had in his name in the years before his death, and he wanted to know why I wanted to know. Remember, we were both talking about a man dead for 65 years.

But I was just as evasive as he was: I told him the McParlands and Campbells had a relationship that went back more than a hundred years -- a personal relationship -- and I wanted to know what additional certificates McParland had other than certificates #11026, 11036, 11070, 6986, 13148, 4476, 8957, 12741, and 3187.

The telephone company executive wanted to know how I knew about these certificates, and I was evasive about that -- saying that I knew they were in McParland's family after he died.

I got nowhere, of course. I got no information at all. But I did get the distinct impression that he knew a great deal more about McParland's finances than he was telling me about, and I wondered what was in that file he had on McParland.

Before he hung up he told me he would consider my request if I sent him a detailed letter explaining why I had to have that information.

I could of course have done that, but I doubted if my explanation of my need would pry the information loose, so I put this issue away in a file with the Hotel Cecil issue, in a file captioned "To be pursued at a later date."

* * * *

Next I turned my attention to Mrs. Tebo and Mrs. Sammons, both of whom had the same address: 3625 Pine Grove Avenue, Chicago.

I bought a street map of Chicago, located 3625 Pine Grove Avenue, and then from the Chicago telephone directory identified the nearest Catholic church to that address -- St. Patrick's.

I wrote to the church and asked if there were any Tebos and Sammons in the congregation who had once lived at 3625 Pine Grove Avenue. I noted that the current Chicago directory did not have any Tebos or Sammons at that address.

I got a reply that Pine Grove Avenue had undergone a change in recent decades -- that minorities lived in that area now, and that the Tebo and Sammon's descendants probably lived elsewhere in the city.

I was at a fork in the road that offered me a choice of direction in pursuing my investigation. I could pursue the Tebo-Sammons connection, as they were the heirs of Mary H. McParland, who in turn was the heir of James McParland, or I could turn my attention to Catherine McParland Murphy, probably a niece of James McParland, who at this point might be still alive.

I filed the Tebo-Sammons lead away with the Mountain States Telegraph and Telephone Company lead and the Hotel Cecil lead, and instead focused my investigation on another person: Catherine McParland Murphy.

A new phase to the investigation then got underway.

CHAPTER FOURTEEN

Who is Catherine McParland Murphy?

I had no idea initially how I was going to go about finding information about Catherine McParland Murphy, but I hoped that if I were methodical enough I would locate her.

After all, I had began investigating James McParland in 1977 with a cold trail that had ended in Mauch Chunk in 1877 -- 100 years before -- and with no information other than that he died in Denver in 1919.

After five years of on-again, off-again research, I had found his last residence, his grave, the place where he had died, two wives, one daughter, three brothers, and a niece in the old homestead over in Armagh. So I was quite confident that with a trail that ended in 1929 -- only 53 years back -- that somehow, some way I would find Catherine McParland Murphy,

After giving the problem some thought, I sent a batch of letters off to various agencies in Chicago inquiring if there were street directories available for Chicago for 1930 and 1935. I thought I would see just how many Catherine Murphys were there and at what address they were located.

I was aware, of course, that Catherine Murphy might be listed under her husband's name, and I did not know what his first name was so this could be a problem. That and the fact that Murphy would probably have scores of listings because it was a common Irish name in a city with a huge Irish population.

I should note that street directories -- listing where people lived -- predated the telephone directory which is now the most common method of locating people, but back in the '20s and '30s few people had phones, so the street directory was the reference most commonly used.

When I was writing away for the Murphy listings for these years, I also wrote away for street directory listings for the name McParland, for 1878, 1880, 1885 and 1900, as well as for 1920, 1925 and 1930, to see if I could locate one of the other McParland brothers, or their descendants.

For a small fee I acquired copies of the requested directories, including telephone directories, for McParland and Murphy for the years I had specified. I then went over them to see what information I could extract from them.

81

The Murphy listings were not of much value -- there were just too many of them and I could spend years eliminating the names one by one.

I had more luck with McParland. The name was not that common -- there were 25 Murphys for every McParland -- so right away I was looking at a very short list.

James McParland, whose occupation was listed as detective, was listed as owning a home at 146 Menominee in Chicago in 1879, and the fact that it was there at all, in a public directory, gave me food for thought.

Here was a man who had helped execute 20 of his fellow countrymen in 1877 and 1878 and who supposedly had made a mortal enemy out of a "terrorist" organization like the Molly Maguires, and yet his home address was printed in a public directory, right after the executions. Obviously, anyone could have found him if they wanted him.

In spite of all the hype about how much danger McParland was in from the Molly Maguires it did not look as if he was in any danger at all, or else why would his home address be listed?

James McParland disappeared from the Chicago directory after 1880 -- presumably to go off and spy on miners out in the Denver area.

In the 1925 directory I came upon a number of McParland listings that interested me because the names matched those I had been looking for.

One was Catherine McParland, listed as living at 5011 Grand Avenue, the same address listed in the Mary McParland will, another was Charles, listed as living at 5011 Grand Avenue, but having a real estate business at 1935 Leclaire, then there was Eneas listed as living at 5011 Grand and having a business address at 1932 Leclaire, and a Nathinal, living at 5011 Grand.

Charles McParland could, of course, be James McParland's brother, and Catherine McParland could be the person I was looking for, and the names Eneas and Nathinal were also interesting, because Mrs. Toner over in Armagh had told me that the Eneas was her father's name and that it was used in every generation of the McParland family. She also told me that the name Nathinal was also a McParland family name, and here I had both of these names listed as living with Charles and Catherine McParland. I believed I was on the right track.

Next, I decided to examine my copy of the current Chicago telephone directory and, perhaps, call every Murphy in the book, hoping that somewhere along the way I would come up with Catherine Murphy -- or one of her descendants.

But one look at the columns of Murphys was enough to tell me that I had a problem on my hands. I was also aware that Catherine McParland Murphy could have moved out of Chicago after her marriage so that I would in reality be wasting my time searching for her in the directory.

After looking at all the Murphys for a time I flipped the pages back to the McParland listing and struck gold right away. There was a McParland listed at 5011 Grand Avenue, the same street address that Charles McParland had had in 1925, only this was a listing for the law office of a John McParland.

On impulse, I dialed the number and asked to speak to John McParland and having introduced myself I told him I was a writer with the *Irish Echo* newspaper and that I was doing research into James McParland, the Pinkerton detective, and I asked him if he were from the same family. He said he was -- that he was the grandson of Charles McParland -- but that he did not know a great deal about his granduncle Jim and that I should talk to his aunt Kitty, who was the family historian, and he gave me her telephone number. She turned out to be the Catherine McParland Murphy I had been looking for.

As soon as I called her up I knew I would have been wasting my time looking for her under the name Murphy, as her married name now was Schick. I do not know what happened to the Murphy name, as I did not ask her.

I then began a long telephone conversation with Kitty Schick, a warm outgoing woman, who talked to me at length about her father Charles and her uncles Jim, Edward, and Frank, and who spoke of all of them with affection.

I did not tell her that I was Alec Campbell's grandnephew, because I thought she would not talk to me freely if I did, and this failure on my part to give her this information caused me a number of guilt trips -- and still does every time I think of that warm old lady in Chicago.

I talked to Kitty Schick four times, and on each occasion I talked to her for about an hour and a half and I also exchanged a number of letters with her to get her impressions of her famous uncle.

Almost immediately she cleared up the mystery of the Hotel Cecil: she said it was in Wellington, New Zealand, and that her uncle Frank had gone out there in the 1880s. She said that Frank kept up a correspondence with Jim right up to the time of his death, and Frank had sent a son over to live with Jim, after Jim's wife and child had died in Denver.

Kitty Schick had also gone out to Denver and lived with her uncle Jim after the New Zealand nephew had been killed in a street accident and she spoke with affection of what she described as Jim's positive qualities.

She was a little evasive on the question of the Molly Maguires, saying that uncle Jim had said they were very bad men, but that he personally had always been against capital punishment and regretted the executions. But she said that Jim was very emphatic that all were guilty of the charges leveled against them and did not regret his part in their conviction.

However, at one point she told me how her uncle, towards the end of his life, was afraid that the relatives of the Molly Maguires would come back one day to get him and that he lived in fear of this.

I thought it ironic, as I listened to her, that McParland was half right -- that a relative of a dead Molly was coming back to get him, but was doing so long after his death.

I could not get any information at all out of her about McParland's finances, and I could not ask her directly, as any attempt I made in this area was rebuffed.

After the first two conversations, I had found out enough about the New Zealand McParlands to launch a Pacific investigation, and also having learned the year of her father's death -- 1928 -- I wrote away to Cook County Probate Court for a copy of the will of Charles McParland.

Th idea behind this move was to see if James McParland had perhaps given a chunk of his estate to Charles before his death.

But I was to discover that Charles McParland's estate had not gone up for probate either, and there was no record of a will, and it appeared that Charles McParland, like his brother James, had disposed of his assets before he died, and therefore left no information around for investigators like me to uncover years later.

Kitty Schick told me that Charles McParland had been a successful real estate broker in Chicago, and that uncle Jim had helped set him up in business. She said her father had also been a member of the state senate and had served there for years.

All of this was very interesting but I wondered how much it had to do with the Molly Maguire story. James McParland could have set his brother up, but I would have to prove he did so with a bounty he got from the Pinkertons, and the fact that Charles was a successful businessman in Chicago at the turn of the century did not mean that it was Molly Maguire money from 20 years prior to that which had financed him.

Meanwhile the letters I had sent out to Wellington, to the public library, had requested information on a Hotel Cecil that had existed from

1880 onwards and I had also requested any information available on Frank McParland, who had owned the hotel. In addition, I requested names and addresses for all the McParlands presently living in Wellington.

I had not asked Kitty about Edward McParland, the fourth brother, and I made a note to ask her about him the next time I talked to her.

I did not have too long to wait before I got a letter back from Wellington's Turnbull Library with a great deal of printed material on the Hotel Cecil and about Frank McParland, its owner.

Among the material was Xeroxed pages of a book entitled "Old Wellington Hotels" which stated that the Cecil was owned by Frank McParland at the turn of the century.

"The Hotel Cecil was known in its heyday as the largest family hotel in the colony. Extending the length of the block, with its picturesque veranda entrance in the centre and its arched doors, the Cecil was the pride of Wellington."

A photograph was included showing the Hotel Cecil, which looked like a New Zealand version of the Waldorf Astoria.

The letter which accompanied the material stated that Frank was listed as the owner of the hotel from 1903 and his two sons, Frank and James, were also in the hotel business, owning the Tramway Hotel in Adelaide Road. An enclosed obituary indicated Frank died in 1911.

The Hotel Cecil had obviously been a very valuable piece of property, seeing it was the "pride of Wellington." And the fact that Pinkerton detective James McParland was able to finance this kind of investment two decades after the Molly Maguire era, after supposedly only making $12 per week as a detective was very interesting. Where would he have got this money, if it were not a bonus for his testimony in the Molly Maguire case? He had been in Denver since 1883, working first as a supervisor and then as manager of the Denver office, but this did not earn him a great deal of money. The manager of the Pinkerton office in Philadelphia, which was far bigger than the Denver office, was only getting $1,500 per year, or $30 per week, back in 1879, so again this was hardly the kind of money that would enable McParland to finance a major purchase abroad, even if McParland increased this salary by the turn of the century to $3,000 per year. This was not enough to finance the purchase of a block-long luxury hotel in New Zealand.

Still, I would have to prove that the money came from a Molly Maguire bonus. He could have been given the money as a gift from some other source. He could have been lucky gambling. He could have struck gold in his spare time. Then again, it probably was the blood money I had been searching for.

In the material I had received from Alexander Turnbull Library I also got a listing of the McParlands in that area and there were just two of them.

I wrote to both and got a reply back from a Mamie McParland, who was the wife of a great-grandson of Frank McParland. I had asked her numerous questions in my letter, including one on the value of the Cecil and how much James McParland had invested in it. But she did not have answers to any of these questions, except that James and Frank had kept up a lifelong correspondence with one another and had seemed very close.

She said that her husband's grandfather, Eneas McParland, had gone out to Denver to live with his uncle Jim after Jim's wife and 12-year-old daughter had died, and that he had married out there while still very young but Eneas and his wife were killed in a traffic accident in Denver, and their two children, Eneas and Frank, who were aged 2 and 4 at the time, were sent back to New Zealand.

This information was not that helpful except it indicated that tragedy had seemed to stalk McParland in Denver: first his wife died suddenly, then his 12-year-old daughter, then this nephew who had come to live with him was killed, as well as the nephew's wife.

* * * *

I had accounted for all of the McParland brothers now except Edward, so I called Kitty Schick back again. I decided I would mention that I had contacted her New Zealand relatives and I also would ask her about some more details on the death of Eneas McParland, as well as on Edward McParland.

On Eneas, she said he had not been doing so well when he lived at home in Wellington -- that he had been a little wild and undisciplined -- and that his father had sent him to James, hoping James would straighten him out.

However, Eneas had still lived in the fast track, even after he married, but nevertheless his death had nothing to do with his lifestyle -- it was just an accident.

She told me Edward McParland had died in a place called Manitou Springs in 1928 and that he had been found dead in bed. She said James had supported Edward financially most of his life, even though he was an "anarchist" who was "really a little off."

I did not pursue the angle on Edward, because I did not see what the "anarchism" of McParland's less affluent brother had to do with the Molly Maguire era and after chatting with her for some time I said good-bye to her, not knowing if I would ever call her again, as I seemed to have got all the information from her that she had.

The Kitty Schick interviews had been very productive as she had given me a score of fascinating anecdotes about McParland's later life, and as I added up all the information that I had received the most valuable part of it was that she had pointed me in the direction of the Hotel Cecil in Wellington, there I had found the probable hiding place for the Molly Maguire bounty.

Kitty Schick was a warm human being and I had another guilt attack as I hung up the phone. But once again, I was aware of the irony of the situation -- here was I using the skills of a detective to try and expose one of the most famous American detectives of all time. I wondered if James McParland, wherever he was, was watching the goings-on back on earth, and if he appreciated my activities.

* * * *

Several days later Kitty Schick called me back and said she had a question to ask me.

"Have you ever been in Pottsville, Pennsylvania?," she said.

I said I had, on numerous occasions.

"You know, I wondered about that," she said, "I used to go down there when I was a child. My grandparents lived on Minersville Road and I used to visit them."

I listened to this statement for a moment and was caught completely off balance. Pottsville was where a dozen of the Mollies had been hanged, and I could not imagine any McParland going within a thousand miles of the place.

"Your grandparents lived in Pottsville?"

"Yes, my mother was from there. Her name was Emile Schoepple -- the family was German."

"And where did your father Charles meet her?"

"Well, originally he met her down there in Pottsville, but my grandparents would not let them marry and he married another girl named Mary Lynch also from down there, but she died and then my mother came to the

World's Fair of 1890 in Chicago and they met again and married. My grandparents never accepted him, but they let me visit Pottsville."

"Didn't your father feel afraid, going back to Pottsville after all those Molly Maguires were executed, and the bitterness still around. I mean, didn't he think it dangerous?" I asked.

"Oh, he did not go down there afterwards -- he and Edward went down there at the same time uncle Jim went down...all three were in the Pinkertons together. Edward and my father also had assumed names -- they went under the maiden name of their mother -- Loughrin -- and their job was to keep close to Jim and warn him if he was in danger of being found out. They kept a very low profile but they were close to him at all times and it was they who warned him to get out of Pennsylvania because the Mollies were on to him."

As she kept talking about the adventures of the three McParland brothers down in Pennsylvania I realized she was handing me the evidence that would have saved Alec Campbell from the gallows -- had it been known at the time. She was also handing me evidence that clearly proved James McParland was an accessory before the fact to the Jones murder.

James McParland had admitted at Alec Campbell's trial that he knew that three men had left Tamaqua and gone to Lansford to kill Jones. He said that he did not go to warn Jones because he was afraid he would be seen doing this by the Mollies and they would kill him. He admitted he could have walked the five miles to Lansford, but said he was afraid to do so -- even thought he had plenty of time: he knew on the evening of September 2 that the murder was to take place on the morning of September 3.

When pressed by Campbell's attorneys why he did not tell the police, or tell some reputable citizen of Tamaqua to go warn Jones, he said he had no one to turn to.

But here was his niece telling me that her father and another uncle were by his side at all times, and it was, therefore, obvious that he had been lying -- he could have sent either one of his brothers over to Lansford to warn Jones. Her revelations also had implications far beyond the Alec Campbell case and the Jones murder: McParland knew in advance of the murders of Gomer James, Bill Thomas, Sanger and Uren, and had used the same excuse for failing to warn the victims -- that he was out of touch with the Pinkertons and that he had no one to turn to.

Obviously, had the existence of the other McParland brothers been known during the trials, not even a rigged jury could have convicted Alec Campbell -- or any of the other defendants convicted and executed on the basis of James McParland's testimony.

Kitty also told me that Edward McParland was sent out of Pennsylvania and out of the Pinkertons during the Mollie trials because he was " a bit of an anarchist."

When I asked her what that meant she said that he was "kind of taking the side of the Mollies, and uncle Jim couldn't put up with that."

However even though he was sent away, she said Jim took care of him all his life.

I asked her what the Schoepples had against her father, Charles, and she said that they "did not like what uncle Jim was doing."

I asked her to be more specific but she would not. She said they just did not like the McParlands and refused to let Emile marry Charles. The thought occurred to me, of course, that the Schoepples had known that James McParland was committing perjury and that he was sending twenty men to the gallows and scores to jail, and that that was reason enough not to like him. But I did not say that to her.

The thought also occurred to me that the Schoepples knew James McParland was lying and they could have told the media, but instead kept quiet, and let Alec Campbell and the others hang. But I did not say anything about that to her either.

What would be the point in confronting this old lady with such unpleasant revelations?

But I did know that all who knew about the existence of those other McParlands during the trials bore some responsibility for what happened on the gallows afterwards.

This new information I had received changed the whole focus of my investigation. I had been planning to try and track Frank McParland's movements in New Zealand, to see if I could determine when he first became affluent, and I was prepared to spend all the time it took on this activity.

I was also going to investigate Charles McParland's business activities in Chicago, from 1878 onwards to see what I could find out that would suggest receiving a bonanza.

I was going to go to Denver and comb the city records to find out just how much property James McParland owned, apart from 1256 Columbine Street, and I was also going to follow up on the beneficiaries in Mary H. McParland's will; namely, the Tebo family and the Sammons family, to see what I could find about them.

And I was going to investigate Edward McParland's life to see what I could find out about him, apart from the fact he died alone in his house at 226 Ruxton Avenue, Manitou Springs, Colorado, on July 3, 1926, at the age of 70.

But now, given the nature of the information I had received from Kitty Schick there did not seem to be any point in going to the trouble to prove James McParland had received a bounty for his Mollie Maguire testimony. After all, the proof about the bounty was to get evidence that James McParland lied about Alec Campbell for a reward, but here I had other more important evidence and I did not need the evidence of bounty money to prove my case.

I did, however, check out Edward McParland and discovered the same pattern of hiding assets that I had discovered in Charles and James. No will. No probate. Married, but wife's name unknown. And the street number on the death certificate, 226 Ruxton Avenue -- did not exist. Those McParland brothers had certainly gone to great lengths to cover up their tracks, even fifty years after the Molly era.

The last item of information I got from Kitty Schick -- about the German-American parents from Pottsville -- helped explain why Robert Pinkerton had been so spooked by the Sherlock Holmes mystery, *The Valley of Fear*. Pinkerton did not like the fact that McParland was characterized in the novel as having married a German girl from Pottsville. It was Charles who married the German girl, not James, but Pinkerton must have disliked how close the novel was getting to the truth.

CHAPTER FIFTEEN

Death of Padraic

The information from the Kitty Schick interviews had opened up the possibility of clearing Alec Campbell completely by providing positive proof that James McParland had been the liar that Mrs. Alec Campbell had said he was.

But I had to document the fact that he had lied on the witness stand at Campbell's trial -- lied when he said he was all alone down in Pennsylvania and had no way of warning John Jones that he was about to be killed.

In order to this I would have to get a verbatim transcript of the trial -- and as luck would have it I learned that all the verbatim transcripts of all the Molly Maguire trials in Carbon County had recently been discovered in the basement of the court house in Jim Thorpe (Mauch Chunk) and copies of them were being made available for a small fee from the Pennsylvania Historic and Museum Commission in Harrisburg.

I wrote away for the verbatim trial transcripts for Alec Campbell's trial for both the Jones and the Powell murders and I received them within two weeks.

The documents in the Jones trial ran to about 1,500 pages, and the Powell trial transcripts numbered over 400 more, and as a result I had almost 2,000 pages of handwritten testimony to go over.

I was determined to go over them very carefully, however, word by word, and to find and document any McParland testimony in the trial where he had told an outright lie.

In the fall of 1985, as I was preparing a methodical search of the mountain of paper that comprised the verbatim transcripts, I became the victim of the most terrible tragedy that can happen to a parent: my thirteen-year-old son Padraic was killed by a hit-and-run driver who struck him while he was crossing the street and left him to die in the gutter.

Nothing prepares a parent for the death of a child and no horror equals it when it happens. The sudden rupture of the family, with a child alive and happy one moment and lying dead on the street the next moment, is catastrophic and is almost beyond endurance.

My world collapsed around me...around my wife Eileen..and around our eight-year-old daughter Nora, and we were left to cope with this agony, which creates a pain that is almost unbearable.

My son had been crossing the street on a skateboard, against the light, and the driver of the car involved had been speeding -- some witnesses said he had been doing 60 miles per hour in a thirty-five mile per hour zone. My son had either not seen the oncoming car, or had misjudged its speed, and paid for it with his life.

The driver slowed down after hitting my son, then sped away, and fled through the Holland Tunnel to New York. But an anonymous tip to the police tracked him down -- and he was charged only with leaving the scene of the accident. The police said they did not have enough evidence to charge him with vehicular homicide. He got thirty days in jail, and was allowed to serve his time on weekends, so that his life would not be too disrupted. My wife, my daughter and I got a life sentence of grief.

This happened just before Christmas in 1985, and although I managed to cope with my normal work routine afterwards, it was five years -- not until November 1990, that I once again picked up on the Alec Campbell story. Until then I had been too busy coping with pain to have the slightest interest in the McParland investigation, and all the material I had assembled lay there in boxes in a closet along with the hundreds of mass cards we had received.

But the passage of time has enabled me to make a new beginning, and even though neither I nor my wife or Nora will ever forget Padraic or the terrible tragedy of his death, we have moved onwards and try to live out the rest of our lives as best we can.

The death of Padraic and the horrifying grief we felt -- and still feel -- has given me an insight into the effects of violent death on surviving family members.

I knew how Alec Campbell's wife and sisters must have felt. I knew the grief his parents had experienced over in Dungloe. And I knew the agony of the Jones family, the Uren family, the Sanger family, and every other family who had become victims of murder.

And I was equally sympathetic to all of them. Without exception.

CHAPTER SIXTEEN

The Alec Campbell Trial for the Murder of Jones

When I took the verbatim trial transcripts out of the storage boxes in the fall of 1990, I decided to examine the 1,500 pages of the Jones trial first, and examine the 400 page of the Powell trial later.

I decided that I was going to go through all the material methodically -- first taking an inventory of what I had on hand and then reading every word on every page.

The trial of Alec Campbell for the murder of John P. Jones was the instrument used to send Campbell to the gallows and therefore every word uttered in this trial was important. In addition, it was the testimony given at the trial that was the basis for the books and articles which focused on the Campbell case and I knew I was going to the source by reading these transcripts. All else was secondary material.

My original plan had been to scan through the trial material until I came to the testimony of James McParland and then go through his testimony until I found where he had committed perjury by swearing there was no way he could have warned John P. Jones that he was in danger of losing his life. I would then use this testimony to point out that McParland had two brothers in the area and he could have sent them to warn Jones. This in turn would destroy McParland's credibility as a witness against Alec Campbell.

But during the long years I had spent investigating McParland I had consistently wasted a great deal of time starting off with erroneous assumptions, and it was only after I had been sidetracked for a long period that I discovered my error. My assumption that McParland had never married, based on several published sources, was an example of this; my long search for the Hotel Cecil in the United States based on my conversation with Mrs. Toner over in Armagh was another. So, I wanted to avoid this kind of thing in my examination of the verbatim trial transcripts.

In order to focus on what assumptions I was bringing to this examination -- assumptions which might be erroneous -- I decided to jot down what exactly I thought was the basic plot of the entire Molly Maguire story.

The summary of my basic assumptions was as follows:

Gowen wanted to break the miners union and the Ancient Order of Hibernians and he hired the Pinkertons, including the McParlands to help him. The Pinkertons either staged or took advantage of murders to frame union and AOH leaders, and Alec became the victim of this conspiracy. Gowen, Allan Pinkerton and James McParland were the prime movers in the conspiracy.

This assumption fitted perfectly with all I had learned so far, but I held this assumption with caution as I began the examination -- prepared to revise that assumption any time, if new information emerged.

So, I resisted the impulse to go to the McParland testimony first in order to document his committing perjury and instead began an inventory and examination of all of the documents that had been generated by the Jones trial.

The documents I had on hand consisted of 1,500 pages of trial transcripts of the Jones trial, including the examination of the jurors, as well as scores of other documents, including Campbell's death warrant, notices of appeal to the Pennsylvania Supreme Court, an appeal to Governor Handranft, and six letters, including one from my great grandparents in Dungloe, dated March 6, 1877, which was a character testimonial for their son.

As I examined all these documents, I saw that hundreds of people were involved in the process that sent Campbell to the gallows, including witnesses, jurors, police, judges, lawyers, jailers, politicians, and eventually the executioner.

Some of these people played only a minor role, like a witness who was on the stand for three minutes, while others like the prosecutor, judge, jury and executioner played a major role.

The first thing I did before I even began to read the trial transcripts was to make up a who-is-who list of all of those heavily involved in the trial, and this was achieved by a careful reading of all of the supporting documents to the trial transcripts.

The presiding judge was Samuel S. Dreher, whom I had heard of before, but I also discovered in these documents the names of James Houston and Levi Weritz, who were listed as associate judges. I scanned the testimony and the summations but could find only Dreher playing an active role and the names of the other two were not even mentioned again.

Before I went on to the next name on my list I decided to go through the books I had accumulated to see what I could find out about Dreher. I discovered he was described as a "hanging" judge who had practiced outside of Carbon County, but had been brought in to preside over the trials by Asa Packer, the Mauch Chunk multimillionaire who owned Mauch Chunk, as well as a score of coal mines and the Lehigh Valley Railroad.

The involvement of Asa Packer in the Campbell trial interested me, but should not have surprised me. Asa Packer was one of the wealthiest men in America and had vital business interests in the anthracite regions. Indeed, he had more at stake in defeating the unions and the AOH than Franklin Gowen, because he actually owned the mines and railroads, whereas Gowen was only a company employee who had been appointed president. Packer had a huge mansion on the side of the hill overlooking the Carbon County Courthouse -- a mansion that still exists -- and he must have taken a very deep interest in the trial.

Remembering my assumption that it had been Franklin Gowen who had been the prime mover in the war on the Mollies, I wondered if Gowen had had a silent partner in Packer, who chose the shadows and let Gowen strut in the limelight.

The district attorney who prosecuted Alec Campbell was E. R. Siewers, but Siewers seems to have taken a back seat throughout the trial to General Charles Albright, who helped select the jury...asked 95 percent of the questions at the trial...and appeared in court in his military uniform, which he had worn during the Civil War.

Albright had a huge town house in Mauch Chunk and mixed socially with Asa Packer, even though he was employed by Charles Parrish.

Charles Parrish, of course, had as much reason to hate the miners union and the AOH as Asa Packer or Franklin Gowen, because he, like Packer, had a huge personal fortune at stake that could be jeopardized by striking miners.

In spite of having a vested interest in defeating the AOH and the Union, Packer was able to appoint a hanging judge who was a personal friend to preside over the Campbell trial and Parrish was able to appoint Albright the chief prosecutor, and in the Pennsylvania legal system of the 1870s this seemed perfectly legitimate as there was no adverse publicity about these appointments.

The next person I scrutinized was assistant prosecutor Allen Craig, who turned out to be Asa Packer's chief counsel, and an employee of the Lehigh Railroad.

The third prosecutor was F. W. Hughes, counsel for Franklin Gowen's Reading Railroad and noted anti-Irish bigot and drunk.

Thus, the entire prosecution team, as well as Judge Dreher, were cronies of the three most powerful moguls in the area: Asa Packer, Franklin

Gowen and Charles Parrish. I wondered if Alec Campbell realized the danger he was in.

Campbell's attorneys were named Daniel Kalbfus, Martin Lavelle and John Fox. Fox and Lavelle were Pottsville lawyers, Kalbfus was the most prominent lawyer in Mauch Chunk and had among his clients many of the town's prominent business leaders. I wondered why Campbell had selected Kalbfus to head his defense and as I began to go through the trial transcripts I thought the selection of Kalbfus was a serious mistake.

The documents also revealed Campbell was arrested by Sheriff Bessimer of Carbon county, who told Campbell he was on the way to the gallows. But Bessimer was dead before Campbell, having died in August 1876, and he was succeeded by a Sheriff Butler whose name vanished in 1877 when the name Sheriff Raudenbush made its appearance. It was Raudenbush who hanged Campbell.

The two other names which I considered important before I began to read the trial transcripts were James Kerrigan and James McParland. But as I began to go through the trial transcripts names like Linden, Franklin, Shepp, Zehner, Walton, Guss, Beard and Halvey became important, and I was to conclude later that they played as important a role in the trial as James McParland had, but neither the media of the time or historians since then seemed to have paid much attention to them.

CHAPTER SEVENTEEN

Jury Selection; The Trial Begins

The first day and a half of the trial was devoted to the selection of the jury, and the way the jury was selected was an indication of how the trial was going to be conducted.

Every Irish Catholic among the 62 jurors impanelled was objected to by the prosecution and the objection was sustained. Thus, no Irish Catholics were on the jury.

The jurors who were selected were either German or Welsh, and three of the Germans could barely speak English, but were allowed to serve anyway. When Campbell's lawyers objected to some of the jurors, their objections were sometimes sustained but often overruled.

Thus, the Campbell lawyers had to watch as a jury was selected whose members were traditionally hostile to the Irish. I do not know what options Kalbfus had to combat the way the jury was selected, but with a hostile judge, three hostile prosecutors and then a hostile jury on board he must have known his client was in deep trouble from the very beginning.

I wondered just what the prosecution case was like, if the prosecution had gone to such lengths to stack the court against Campbell before the trial even began.

The testimony itself ran for seven days and was divided into phases.

The first phase included the testimony of scores of witnesses who saw Edward Kelly, Michael Doyle and James Kerrigan before and after the murder of John Jones in and around Tamaqua and Lansford. Kelly, Doyle and Kerrigan were the three who carried out the murder; Campbell was accused of being an accessory, although he was not at the scene of the crime.

The second phase was the testimony of James Kerrigan, who had turned state's evidence in order to save his neck, and who implicated Campbell in the plot to kill Jones.

Kerrigan was an infamous witness, however, and his testimony could not stand alone, and so James McParland was introduced as the supporting witness who confirmed Kerrigan's testimony and thereby put a rope around Campbell's neck. The defense lawyers tried to portray McParland as an infamous witness also, but the lawyers seemed not to know what I

97

knew about McParland's two brothers, and McParland did very well for the prosecution in his two days of testimony.

The next phase was a re-examination of many of the witnesses, and the final phase was a parade of defense witnesses who contradicted most of the testimony of the prosecution witnesses.

As I began to read the testimony of witnesses in the first phase I was amazed at the sheer numbers of witnesses who had seen Michael Doyle, Edward Kelly and James Kerrigan in Lansford on the two nights before the murder. Witnesses placed them near where Jones worked, where he lived, and outside of Alec Campbell's house. The weight of this evidence was overwhelming, and unless 60 different people were persuaded to lie and then did not contradict one another, it would seem conclusive that these men were at the scene of the crime and were also in the vicinity of Campbell's hotel.

The majority of these witnesses of course had already testified in the trial of Edward Kelly and Michael Doyle and their testimony had helped get the pair a death sentence.

However, as I was reading the testimony I began to sense that there was something wrong with it -- although I could not determine at first what exactly was wrong because the testimony seemed so straightforward and unambigious. But I had this intuition about the testimony as a whole, and about the testimony of several of the witnesses in particular, and I stopped reading any further and decided not to begin reading phase two -- the testimony of James Kerrigan -- until I had put a finger on what was disturbing me.

The first witness whose testimony had made me pause was the testimony of Ann Halvey, who said she saw Kelly and Doyle outside of the Jones house on September 2, the night before the murder. She lived next door to Jones and she said Kelly asked her 4-year-old son if Jones was at home. The next witness whose testimony raised some questions was Elizabeth Halvey, the daughter of Ann Halvey, who said she saw Jones working alone in his backyard early that evening and that she had seen him go off to work at 7:00 a.m. the following morning, walking alone down the hill toward Lansford station as he did every day. Several minutes after she saw him he was ambushed and shot on the hillside by Kerrigan, Doyle and Kelly.

I read their testimony several times and tried to determine what it was that bothered me so much about it. I knew that there had to be a discrepancy here between his testimony and something I had read before and that my subconscious was picking up on it. I was right.

When I went back to my files to where I had made notes that I had jotted down from various books about the actual killing of John P. Jones I found several notes that made reference to Jones being guarded by the Coal and Iron Police, after the Pinkertons had warned him there was a plot on his life.

Yet Mrs. Halvey had made no mention of the police guarding her next-door neighbor and her daughter's testimony that Jones was out alone in his backyard while the killers were out front seemed at odds with him having been warned he was in danger of assassination. The fact that he went off to work alone, unarmed and unguarded, also seemed at odds with the testimony that he was aware of a plot on his life.

I still, however, had the feeling that that was not the only thing about the Halvey evidence that I found disturbing, and I read it and read it again for days, until suddenly one evening I got an insight not only into why the testimony of the Halveys was disturbing me so much, but why the entire first phase of the testimony had made me feel ill at ease as well. And the insight came when I was going through my notes and came across a reference to the murder of Tamaqua policeman Benjamin Yost, which James Kerrigan was also involved in and played a role similar to that which he played in the Jones killing.

Kerrigan's role in the Yost murder had been dealt with at length in the Wayne Broehl book on the Molly Maguires, and Broehl had described how Kerrigan had led two gunmen from Lansford, Hugh McGeehan and James Boyle, up Broad Street in Tamaqua and ambushed police office Yost as he stood beside a lamp post.

The killing was conducted at night and Kerrigan remained in the shadows so he would not be recognized while the two gunmen shot Yost. The whole modus operandi employed by Kerrigan in the Yost killing was to move quietly on darkened streets so that the gunmen would not be recognized and then strike quickly from the shadows, before vanishing into the night.

Yet the same Kerrigan had brought two gunmen to Lansford on a similar mission, but instead of darkness, secrecy and a quick strike from the shadows, he paraded his associates up and down the streets of Lansford in broad daylight for two days before the killing, being recognized before the murder by scores of people, including the Halveys and the sisters of Jones, and then, after the murder, led the pair back to Tamaqua, instead of hiding out in the hills, and walked them into the arms of the police.

The aspect of the first phase of the testimony that had been bothering my subconscious was that there were just too many good witnesses -- that even the most incompetent gunman would have taken some precaution not to be recognized by potential witnesses, and yet this Kerrigan, who was supposedly a shrewd little desperado, had acted as if he was setting himself and his associates up to get caught. The whole thing just did not make any sense.

As I mulled over the possible reasons why Kerrigan behaved the way he did, I read once again the testimony of three other witnesses whose evidence had struck a wrong note with me. One was the testimony of Samuel Beard, another was the testimony of Michael Beard, and the third was the testimony of Wallace Guss.

The Beard name was of particular interest to me because I had read in the Broehl book that Michael Beard was a member of a Tamaqua Vigilante Committee who had hired the Pinkertons to track down the killers of Yost. Broehl had also found a memo in the Pinkerton files which stated that Michael Beard had not only been informed on August 5 that James Kerrigan had participated in the murder of police officer Yost but was also involved in a plan to murder mine boss Jones.

So, the two Beards who testified at the Alec Campbell trial -- Michael and Samuel, who were father and son -- were well aware before the Jones killing that there was a plan to kill Jones and they also knew that James Kerrigan was very much involved in it.

Given this, it was more than a little bizarre that Samuel Beard said he just happened to be on the Tamaqua-Lansford train at 7:30 a.m. on September 3 and was at the Lansford station when Jones was shot.

Samuel Beard said he was on his way to Mauch Chunk that morning and that he had just happened to hear about the shooting when the train pulled into Lansford.

Beard made no mention that he had been aware of a plot to kill Jones and he made no mention of the fact that he knew Kerrigan was a prime mover in it.

And the prosecution attorneys did not bring this up, and neither did the defense lawyers, although they all knew about it.

Beard left the train and went to the dying John P. Jones and then went back to Tamaqua on a special train to spread the word about the Jones killing.

Samuel Beard's actions in the next two hours were even more bizarre. He testified that he went to his office for two hours to work and then at

10:00 a.m. he and a friend took a spyglass -- binoculars -- and went up to the Odd Fellows Cemetery, where he looked down the valley and saw James Kerrigan near the cemetery with Doyle and Kelly.

Beard's testimony poses several questions: where was he going in the morning on the Mauch Chunk train if his mission was so unimportant that he returned to Tamaqua and went to work after the Jones killing? Why did he stay exactly two hours at work, before heading up to the Odd Fellows Cemetery with his spy glass -- just in time to see James Kerrigan arrive with Doyle and Kelly? How did he suspect the killers would come in that direction -- it was a two-hour walk from Lansford -- when they could have gone in any one of a dozen other directions?

The defense showed no interest in Samuel Beard's testimony and did not ask what seemed to me to be the obvious questions: "How did you know that James Kerrigan would bring the gunmen back to Tamaqua? How were you able to time your departure from your office so precisely that you were in the right place at the right time to see Kerrigan, Doyle and Kelly? Why did you not mention that you had advance knowledge that Kerrigan was involved in the plot?"

The testimony of the other Beard -- Michael Beard -- was very brief. He said he owned a hotel and that the Tamaqua jail was at the rear of his hotel, in his back yard. He said the prisoners were brought there and locked up. His testimony made no reference to the fact that he had hired the Pinkertons to find out who had killed Yost, and the prosecution did not bring it up. Neither did the defense lawyers -- who could have brought out the fact that he had known for a month who was involved in the Jones plot.

The next witness who gave me food for thought was Wallace Guss, a close friend of Michael Beard and also a member of the Tamaqua Committee. It was Guss who had, with the help of Samuel Beard, actually arrested Kerrigan, Doyle and Kelly.

Guss described the arrest of Kerrigan, Doyle and Kelly and also described how he treated Kerrigan in a manner very different from the way he treated Doyle and Kelly.

After telling Kelly and Doyle that they had better come quietly or else they would be gunned down, he told Kerrigan that it was the other two he was after, and he treated Kerrigan as if he were a friend.

When the prisoners were brought down Broad Street to the prison at the rear of Beard's Hotel he made Doyle and Kelly strip and he examined all their clothing, but he did not ask Kerrigan to strip, and looked in only two of his vest pockets.

Campbell attorney Fox asked:

Q:"Had you heard of the murder of Jones at this point?"
A: "Yes, sir."
Q: "Before you went out?"
A: "Yes. I heard Jones had been shot."
Q: "Then you did not examine Kerrigan's clothes or stockings nor anything of that sort?"
A: "No, sir, from the fact I did not think he was in it"

Guss was obviously lying here and Fox knew it. Guss and his friend Michael Beard had known since August 5 that Kerrigan had killed Yost and was planning to kill Jones, and Guss was saying under oath that he did not search Kerrigan because he did not think he "was in it."

What grounds did he have for thinking James Kerrigan was not involved? What grounds did he have for thinking Kelly and Doyle were? The arrest had happened within hours of the shooting and no witnesses had come from Lansford to identify the killers.

In spite of this Fox did not pursue this line of questioning and while he skirmished mildly with both Guss and Michael Beard, he really did not go after them where they were most vulnerable, namely in their kid glove treatment of James Kerrigan at the time of his arrest.

This special treatment of James Kerrigan at the time of his arrest suggests that an understanding had been reached with Kerrigan before the murder of Jones, because there had been no time or opportunity to reach this understanding between the time of the murder and the arrest. Kerrigan, in his testimony, reinforced this by boasting how well his friend Guss treated him when he was arrested. Obviously, Kerrigan had turned state's evidence before the Jones killing, not after he was arrested and charged with the murder of Jones.

The testimony of the Halveys, the Beards and that of Wallace Guss had raised a whole new set of questions about the Jones murder. And the inexplicable behavior of the defense lawyers raised even more questions.

I did not know how to evaluate this testimony and did not know what exactly to make of it at that point.

I had begun to read the verbatim trial transcripts with the theory that there had been a Gowen-Pinkerton-McParland plot to do in Alec Campbell, and here I was in the first two days of the trial with Asa Packer and Charles Parrish playing leading roles in the prosecution, and several prosecution witnesses giving evidence that suggested that there was a great deal more to the Jones murder than that which had been reported in the newspapers of the day or published in the books on the Molly Maguires.

The major questions posed by the testimony in the first phase were the following: why had James Kerrigan exposed himself and Kelly and Doyle to scores of witnesses; why did the two Beards and Wallace Guss treat Kerrigan so nicely when they knew he had just killed John P. Jones? Why did the Halveys see no evidence that Jones was being guarded; and above all why did Alec Campbell's lawyers not exploit all of these opportunities to weaken the prosecution case?

CHAPTER EIGHTEEN

Introducing James Kerrigan

James Kerrigan was on the witness stand on June 23, the third day of testimony and his testimony was as important as James McParland's in sending Alec Campbell to the gallows. Indeed, Wallace Guss said after the trials were all over that without Kerrigan's help the majority of the Mollie Maguires would never have been convicted.

Kerrigan came to the witness stand admitting that he had been with the men who killed Yost, and the men who killed Jones. He came to the witness stand accused by his own wife of being the one who shot Yost -- and she also swore he acted alone because he hated Yost and that Boyle and McGeehan had nothing to do with it.

The story told by Kerrigan was that he had been sworn into the Molly Maguires in 1871 by Alec Campbell and that Alec Campbell was the one who had set up the murders of Yost, Jones and Morgan Powell.

He said Campbell had Powell killed in 1871 because Powell discriminated against Campbell because of his nationality and that Campbell set up the murder of Yost in exchange for arranging the killing of Jones. Jones was slated for death because he was supposed to have blacklisted union organizer Hugh McGeehan and prevented him from getting any work in the mines.

The deal Campbell had worked out was that Hugh McGeehan and James Boyle, another Campbell friend, go to Tamaqua where they met Kerrigan, and he, in turn, showed them where to ambush police officer Yost as he was making his final rounds for the evening. According to Kerrigan, Yost was killed because he had been giving James Duffy and other Irishmen a bad time. The leader of the AOH in Tamaqua was James Carrol, a saloon owner there, and Carrol was indicted on murder charges for the killing of Yost, and so were Duffy, James Roarity, McGeehan and Boyle. Campbell had not been charged in this killing.

After Yost had been killed, Campbell demanded, according to Kerrigan, that Carrol and Kerrigan find two men who were unknown in Lansford and get them to shoot Jones. Kerrigan said he did this, and claimed he was afraid that Alec Campbell would kill him if he refused.

Kerrigan told his story with a great deal of sincerity and the prosecution went along with it, even though it had in its possession the McParland reports which stated that it was Kerrigan himself who hated Yost and wanted him killed -- not James Duffy. Kerrigan claimed he was giving this testimony not to save his own life but because he had come to the conclusion that Alec Campbell was a very evil person and had to be exposed. He said no deal with the prosecution had been made.

The prosecution strategy, as it was reflected in Kerrigan's testimony, was to tie McGeehan into the plot, because he was supposed to have the motivation, and to tie Alec Campbell into the plot, because he provided the leadership. The fact that the elaborate and obviously incompetent staging of the killing raises questions about whether Kerrigan was telling the truth at all when he implicated McGeehan and Campbell.

And inadvertently he weakened the prosecution case -- or should have weakened it anyway -- by later saying that it was William Zehner, the chief superintendent of the mines, who had ordered the blacklisting of McGeehan -- not John P. Jones. This eliminated the McGeehan and the Campbell motivation for killing Jones.

The defense lawyers attacked Kerrigan's character and he responded sanctimoniously that he had reformed; they pointed out some minor discrepancies in his testimony, but he stuck to his guns. But they did not question the overall strategy of the plot, which was so obviously designed to get the killers caught, and while they focused on the special privileges Kerrigan was receiving since his incarceration, they did not put the spotlight on why Wallace Guss had treated him so kindly on the day of his arrest, and why Guss said Kerrigan was not involved. Finally, they failed to ask Kerrigan why he had brought the killers back to Tamaqua, instead of heading off into the hills.

Kerrigan was on the stand on June 23 and 24 and he was cocky and self-confident throughout. Although he denied he had made a deal to escape prosecution, he acted throughout the trial like a man who had nothing to fear and who was confident of his own future.

Kerrigan was a big hit with the jury who smiled at his "wiseguy" demeanor on the stand. And Kerrigan enjoyed the spotlight and he preened himself frequently as he watched the reporters take down every word he said.

Kerrigan was also a star in the eyes of the prosecutors, who treated Kerrigan with the deference due a senator, and he was ushered in and out of the witness stand by sheriff's deputies, who accorded him the courtesy normally given to a major celebrity. Of the prosecution team, only

McParland refused to bow to Kerrigan -- in spite of Kerrigan's friendly greetings to McParland and his attempts to insinuate that "Jimmie" was his buddy. It seemed that informer McParland did not respect informer Kerrigan very much.

Alec Campbell listened to Kerrigan's testimony with his expression reflecting rage and frustration. But he said nothing and remained calm. Mrs. Campbell and Alec's brother and two sisters were obviously furious at Kerrigan, and they told reporters during recesses that Kerrigan was a liar, a drunk and a vicious killer and nobody should believe anything he said.

I gave a great deal of thought to the Kerrigan testimony in the next few days and tried to come up with a theory that would explain his behavior before and after the Jones murder -- a theory which would also resolve all the disturbing testimony in phase one of the trial, including the failure of Alec Campbell's lawyers to take advantage of all of the opportunities offered them.

The only theory that was compatible with all of that was as follows: when McParland told Wallace Guss, the Beards, Gowen, Packer and Parrish that James Kerrigan had murdered Benjamin Yost, they approached Kerrigan and threatened him with the hangman if he did not set up the murder of Jones and accuse Alec Campbell and Hugh McGeehan of being involved in the plot. Kerrigan was following orders when he acquired the gunmen Doyle and Kelly and was following orders when he paraded them up and down the streets of Lansford. He was also following orders when he brought them back to Tamaqua, where the Beards and Wallace Guss were waiting for him.

And where did Alec Campbell's lawyers fit into this? There were two options: one, they were completely incompetent and could not see the obvious; two, they were part of the plot.

Was this a plausible theory? It was possible, anything is possible, but I had no idea whether it was in fact the truth. It definitely seemed far-fetched, since it would mean that Gowen, Packer, Parrish, the Pinkertons and the Tamaqua Committee had deliberately set up an innocent mine boss -- John P. Jones -- in order to get convictions against union and AOH leaders. It would mean that the leaders of the conspiracy had no qualms about whom they killed, as long as they destroyed both the union and the AOH.

Was it possible? I didn't know, and I still do not know, but it remains the only theory I have about the reasons for having Jones killed and Campbell hanged for the murder.

CHAPTER NINETEEN

McParland Takes the Stand

James McParland came on the witness stand after James Kerrigan and he testified for two days and his testimony took up 200 pages of the trial transcripts. He was immaculately groomed and self-possessed throughout.

Here at last was the man I had chased all over Denver, in Chicago, and back in his old home in Armagh, and in these transcripts I would read the testimony which I believed had been responsible for sending Alec Campbell to the gallows.

Given the fact that I had unearthed a great deal of new information from the testimony of the witnesses who had preceeded McParland I was determined to read his testimony with the utmost care and immediately jot down anything that seemed offbeat or contradictory.

James McParland dominated the proceedings on June 25 and 26. His testimony captured the attention of all the major newspapers of the period, including the *New York Times*, the *Tribune*, the *New York World*, the *New York Herald* and scores of other newspapers, including all of the Pennsylvania papers.

McParland mesmerized those who listened to him on the stand. He had a stage presence and was able to keep his audience's complete attention. He described how he was asked by Allan Pinkerton to infiltrate the Mollie Maguires and how he gradually made his way up through the ranks until he was Division President or Body Master of the Shenandoah branch of the Ancient Order of Hibernians.

His was a tale of sabotage, arson and murder, of assignments traded among Body Masters, so that victims never knew the men who shot them down.

McParland testified that he went from town to town in Carbon and Schuylkill counties, using the name James McKenna, pretending to have an abundant supply of counterfeit money which he would spend liberally in saloons patronized by the Mollies. He said he portrayed himself as a hard-drinking, belligerent, violent Irishman, willing to take on a Welsh or English mine boss. According to his testimony he soon became one of the most popular vagabonds in the entire region.

McParland first entered the region in February of 1873 and over the next three years got to know all of the leaders of the AOH in the area. During this time he was sending reports back to Benjamin Franklin almost daily about Mollie activities. In one of these he noted his first meeting with Alec Campbell in June of 1874 at Summit Hill. He described Campbell as a leader in the AOH.

McParland's testimony in the trial has always received a great deal of attention from historians. Many believe that it was designed to convict Campbell as an accessory to murder because of his leadership in the AOH.

The McParland story went as follows: he said that throughout his stay in the coal regions, he discovered that the Ancient Order of Hibernians and the Molly Maguires were one and the same organization. The Molly Maguires were engaged in sabotage, arson and murder against the mine owners. They had a network of cooperating divisions throughout the region with secret signs and passwords and they traded killings. The most powerful men in the Mollies were the Body Masters who controlled the AOH. They were tyrants who were feared by the ordinary members. When a Body Master ordered a killing, the members had to carry it out.

Alec Campbell, according to McParland, was a Body Master of the AOH and, therefore, in this capacity he was up to his ears in violence. Campbell had ordered the killing of Yost and boasted about it to McParland. Campbell had ordered the killing of Jones and boasted about this to McParland too. This testimony confirmed Kerrigan's testimony and it was this testimony that sent Campbell to the gallows.

The American media, which was virulently anti-Irish at the time, had a field day with McParland's tale of secret passwords and a terror network with 6,000 AOH divisions all over the United States and a headquarters in New York, with the supreme headquarters, called the Board of Erin, in Ireland. McParland said the secret passwords came over from Ireland every three months and dues were sent back there. He created the illusion of a vast perverse network of sociopaths, ordering up mayhem whenever they felt like it and killing for very little reason.

Alec Campbell, of course, was a major player: the most intelligent of the leaders in Pennsylvania and also the most cunning and vicious. He had an aura of leadership and could get lesser men to do his will. He was a very bad man indeed, said McParland -- an absolute menace to society.

Day by day, McParland's testimony was dutifully reported in the media as the absolute truth, and Alec Campbell watched as his reputation took on the aura of a monster. There was nothing he could do about it, because he had become the "chieftain among chieftains" and the reputation was to follow his name beyond the grave.

The defense lawyers accused mcParland of being an accessory, because he did not warn Jones, but McParland claimed he had no way of warning Jones, and by giving this testimony he was committing perjury, making him an infamous witness.

At first, I was going to abandon any further analysis of McParland's testimony once I had found him telling the lie about his being unable to warn Jones, since I then had the smoking pistol I had been looking for, but then I thought that since I had come this far, I decided I would not only read all of McParland's testimony but all of the trial transcripts as well.

However, as I ploughed through the mountain of pages of hand-written testimony, which included hundreds of names, dates and accounts of incidents, I became confused by an overload of facts, and this was not helped by the tendency of both the prosecution and the defense to jump back and forth in time, asking McParland to repeat testimony. McParland himself added to the confusion by peppering his testimony with a lot of digressions, which made the testimony even more difficult to follow.

When I then read the testimony of other prosecution witnesses which was supposed to support certain aspects of McParland's testimony, I once again began to sense something far wrong with the prosecution case as my subconscious picked up discrepancies and contradictions. These discrepancies and contradictions did not emerge from McParland's testimony -- the wily detective never contradicted himself once -- but from the testimony of other prosecution witnesses, who were contradicting McParland and each other at every turn.

In order to bring some semblance of order to the mountain of testimony from a score of witnesses, I pinned up on the wall of my den huge 4' x 4' sheets of paper, ten in all, and lined them up side by side.

Then I outlined McParland's key statements on vital issues and arranged these issues in chronological order on the first sheet of paper from top to bottom.

On the other sheets of paper, I listed the testimony of other key prosecution witnesses on the same issues and in the same chronological order, and when I was finished I had two entire walls of my den covered with huge sheets of white paper which enabled me to cross-reference all vital testimony.

It took me two weeks to do this, but when I was finished, I was able to instantly cross-reference all the prosecution testimony and bring order into what had been total chaos.

110

However, my den had now taken on the appearance of a war room, with the testimony of the prosecution witnesses lined up like so many battle plans and me playing the enemy strategist probing all of it for fatal weaknesses.

CHAPTER TWENTY

An Analysis of McParland's Testimony

I began to cross reference dates beginning with McParland's testimony that he met Alec Campbell on July 17 and that Campbell had told him all about the plot against John P. Jones and who was involved in it.

When McParland was asked by the prosecution what steps he had taken to protect the life of Jones once he knew it was being threatened, he said he reported the matter personally to Captain Linden, the Pinkerton agent who was also a captain in the Coal and Iron Police. He said he also wrote a report to Benjamin Franklin, supervisor of the Pinkerton office in Philadelphia. When asked how he knew they had warned Jones, he said Linden had told him.

It must be noted that at this time Yost had already been killed and McParland had, according to himself, been sending in daily reports about the activities of the Molly Maguires -- so there was every reason, if you believe the Pinkertons, to be convinced that Jones' life was in extreme danger and that James Kerrigan, the instigator of the Yost murder, could descend on Jones at any time to kill him.

However, when the testimony of Benjamin Franklin is checked , he said he received the McParland report on July 19, but did not inform anyone until August 5 -- 17 days later -- when he sent a report to Daniel Shepp, a member of the Tamaqua Committee, about the plot to kill Jones, and asked him to warn Jones.

Franklin also said he had heard later that the Committee had informed Captain Williams of the Coal and Iron Police who then put an armed guard on Jones.

The question that must be asked is why the Pinkertons waited 17 days to warn the Committee, given the critical nature of the threat. This becomes even more incriminating when you go back to McParland's testimony and read that Alec Campbell had told him that Kerrigan was going to do the killing on July 27, and that the killing had not occurred then only because Campbell stopped him for tactical reasons. Jones, therefore, could have been killed on July 27, even though the Pinkertons knew all about the plot ten days prior to that, and they did not, according to Franklin's testimony, issue any warnings.

112

Neither the prosecution or the defense asked Franklin for an explanation of the delay. While one can understand why the prosecution would not ask the obvious question, why would the defense not go for another golden opportunity to accuse the Pinkertons of setting up Jones? There is no answer in the trial transcripts and the matter does not seem to have been focused on in other Molly Maguire studies either, or in the newspapers of the day.

There is more, however. The Pinkertons were not the only ones to stall. The Tamaqua Committee itself did not call the police for another week, until August 12. This is 26 days after McParland says he received the warning from Campbell and seven days after the Tamaqua Committee acknowledged receiving the report from the Pinkertons.

The prosecution did not follow Franklin's testimony with that of Daniel Shepp, the Tamaqua Committee leader who received the Pinkerton report. Instead, they brought on two policemen, who verified that they had been told to guard Jones.

The testimony of these policemen is critical and is being given in its entirely here to show the discrepancy between what police officer Walton said and what Captain T. C. Williams, who followed him, said. The key factors to focus on are the timing of the warning to Jones and the steps taken to protect him.

Charles Walton Sworn in on behalf of the Commonwealth. Direct examination by:

Mr. Albright

Q: "Are you a member of the Coal and Iron Police?
A: "Yes, sir."
Q: "State whether or not you knew John P. Jones and whether you did anything to prevent his assassination."
A: "I did know him and I was stationed there for about a week or ten days before he was killed. I was stationed there in the evening to guard the house at night."
Q: "Who sent you there?"
A: "Well, I got my orders from Captain Williams."
Q: "Is he the chief officer there?"
A: "I don't know as he was chief officer; I did not know where he got

the orders from, but it was him that gave them to me."

Q: "Where were you with Mr. Jones?"

Q: "I was at his house."

NO CROSS EXAMINATION

Among the discrepancies are the following: Walton said he was assigned to guard Jones "a week or ten days before he was killed," which would have placed him on duty anytime between August 25 and August 27. He makes no mention of being accompanied by any other policeman.

His supervisor Captain C. Williams, who was on the stand next, said he was told by Daniel Shepp on August 12 and that he immediately went and told Jones at Lansford and also put two men, P.O. Walton and P.O. Sam Ware, in the Jones house to guard him at night. This is 15 days prior to the date given by Walton as being the date he started to guard Jones.

Williams also said that he had the police guard Jones at night until September 1 and then he removed them.

Now, it was known from Kerrigan's testimony that the evening of September 1 was the time he arrived from Tamaqua with two men to kill Jones. The police were apparently pulled out of the Jones house just as Kerrigan arrived in Lansford. It was also known from McParland's report that the killers were going to strike in the open during the day -- not at night. Since the plot was well known, why guard Jones at night and leave him unguarded during the day? And McParland, the following day, made no attempt to warn Jones. He went to bed later that night, leaving Kerrigan a clear field to carry out the murder.

In cross-examining Captain Williams, Kalbfus, Campbell's lawyer, did not ask all the obvious questions about why Jones was guarded at night instead of during the day or why Williams pulled his men out on the evening that Kerrigan arrived. Instead Kalbfus asked only two questions, and they are as follows:

CROSS EXAMINATION BY MR. KALBFUS

Q: "Were your men there on the night of September second?"

A: "That I am not positive of."

Q: "Do you know when they were there last?"

A: "If I am not mistaken, Walton was there either the last night of August or the first night of September."

END OF CROSS EXAMINATION

Next up on the stand was William D. Zehner, superintendent of the Lehigh and Wilkes Barre Coal Co., who was John P. Jones' supervisor. His testimony was in conflict with Franklin's and McParland's on several critical issues and it is worth reading all of his testimony, paying particular attention to names, dates and motivation for the Jones murder.

William D. Zehner, sworn on behalf of the Commonwealth; direct examination by Mr. Albright

Q: "What is your position?"

A: "Superintendent of the Lehigh and Wilkes Barre Coal Company."

Q: "Where?"

A: "Lansford."

Q: "Were you there last August and September?"

A: "Yes, sir."

Q: "State whether or not you received any information from any parties in Tamaqua, and if so state the names of the parties warning you of any dangers to John P. Jones."

A: "I received information to that effect from Mr. Beard of Tamaqua."

Q: "About what time?"

A: "About the first of August, I should judge."

Q: "Did you do anything in consequence of that information to prevent the assassination of Mr. Jones, as far as you could?"

A: "Yes, sir, I did."

Q: "What did you do? What steps did you take?"

A: "Well, I notified Mr. Jones and told him I thought he was in danger and also advised him not to go to the collieries at the upper end of the valley along the old railroad that he had been accustomed to traveling."

Q: "That is the old road going to No. 4?"

A: "Yes, sir, and that he should come to Lansford every morning and go up on the locomotive; that would probably be the safest way."

Q: "Had you any information which led you to believe or suppose that his life was in danger on the old road going to No. 4?"

A: "I had no information; it was merely precaution."

Q: "Did Mr. Beard inform you where he got his information from that he gave you?"

A: "Yes, sir. He said he got it from Mr. Franklin, the superintendent of the Pinkerton Agency, I think."

Q: "Did you know Hugh McGeehan and Tom Mulhall?"

A: "Yes, sir."

Q: "Had they been in the employ of your company?"

A: "They had."

Q: "In July or August, along there, were they discharged or not?"

A: "They were discharged; that is before we resumed work after the strike. I issued orders that those two men should not receive employment at any of our collieries."

Q: "You refused to have them employed?"

A: "Yes, sir."

Q: "Did you know Michael Doyle and Edward Kelly?"

A: "No, sir."

Q: "Were they ever employed at your coal works?"

A: "Not that I know of."

Q: "Didn't know of any such person there?"

A: "No, sir."

Q: "You have seen those two persons have you not -- the defendants?"

A: "I have since their arrest."

Q: "Having seen them in court or elsewhere, do you know of their having been employed in your coal works?"

A: "No, sir."

The first conflict is with a date: Zehner said he was informed by Tamaqua Committee member Beard of the plot on Jones on August 1, four days before Franklin said he mailed out the report on August 5. He also said he told Jones personally of the plot, and this conflicts with Captain Williams, who said Jones was notified for the first time on August 12.

Zehner also stated that it was he, not Jones, who had ordered McGeehan and Mulhall blacklisted and this is confirmed in Kerrigan's testimony. Therefore, the motivation for killing Jones is not clear -- the motivation was there for killing Zehner, who was the one doing the blacklisting.

Finally, Zehner who knew the details of the plot, knew that Kerrigan was the leader of the gunmen and that the attempt on Jones would be made in the morning as he walked to work, yet he did not take steps to guard Jones during the day. Zehner said he just told Jones to watch out.

Campbell's lawyer Daniel Kalbfus did not go after Zehner on any of these discrepancies. Instead, he asked him two questions, both of which were irrelevant:

CROSS EXAMINATION BY KALBFUS

Q: "Was Alec Campbell in your employment at that time?"
A: "No, sir."
Q: "Had he been discharged?"
A: "Not that I know of."

END OF CROSS-EXAMINATION

There was one other conflict in the Zehner testimony with the testimony of other prosecution witnesses and that was with the testimony given by Benjamin Franklin. Franklin said he wrote to Daniel Shepp and told him about the Jones plot and that Shepp told him he had told Charles Parrish, President of the Wilkes Barre Coal and Iron Company. Franklin also said that Shepp had not told anyone else about the plot.

Yet, here is Zehner testifying he had been told by Michael Beard, and prior to Zehner's testimony Captain Williams had testified that Beard had warned him about the Jones plot.

The point is that we have testimony that Charles Parrish, president of the Wilkes Barre Coal and Iron Company, knew of the plot; we have testimony that Zehner, the superintendent of the same company, knew; we have testimony that Captain Williams, who was also an employee of this company, knew; and we can be sure that General Charles Albright, the chief prosecutor of Alec Campbell who was also chief counsel of the Wilkes Barre Coal and Iron Company, knew in advance of the plot. But there is no evidence at all that another company employee, John P. Jones, who was the victim of the plot, knew anything at all about the details of the plot. No proof at all of that was offered by the prosecution.

117

At this point it would be useful to present the crucial dates and names during the 49 days between July 17 and September 4, all compiled from the prosecution's case against Campbell.

<u>July 17</u> McParland said he learned of the Campbell-Kerrigan plot to kill Jones. He said he sent a report on the plot off to Benjamin Franklin, superintendent of the Pinkerton office in Philadelphia.

<u>July 19</u> Franklin said he received the report on that date. Robert Linden, the Pinkerton supervisor in the field, said that he was informed of the plot by McParland in July. He also said McParland had been asked by Campbell to arrange the killing.

<u>July 24</u> Kerrigan was coming to Lansford to kill Jones, but Alec Campbell called it off, according to McParland.

<u>August 1</u> William Zehner said he was told by Michael Beard of the Tamaqua Committee of the Kerrigan-Campbell plot to kill Jones. He said he informed Jones. Discrepancy with Michael Beard and Franklin testimony.

<u>August 5</u> Date of report that Franklin had sent to Daniel Shepp. He said he mailed it. Discrepancy with Zehner.

<u>August 7</u> Michael Beard said he thought he got the report at the end of July, or maybe it was in August -- perhaps the 7. Said he told Daniel Shepp about it and William Zehner, also Charles Parrish.

<u>August 12</u> Captain C. Williams said he heard of plot from Daniel Shepp. Said he told Jones, and immediately put guard on him -- officers Walton and Ware. This was seven days after Shepp heard of the plot.

<u>August 24</u> P.O. Walton said he was placed in Jones home as a guard. This was 12 days after Williams heard of the plot.

<u>September 1</u> Walton removed from Jones house.

<u>September 1</u> Kerrigan, Doyle and Kelly arrive in the Jones neighborhood.

<u>September 2</u> Kerrigan, Doyle and Kelly go all over Lansford and are seen by scores of witnesses.

<u>September 3</u> Jones is shot dead at 7:00 a.m.

<u>September 4</u> McParland meets Campbell, while Campbell is campaigning for an Irish-American politician, and McParland claims Campbell was angry at Kerrigan for making a mess of the job.

There are obvious problems with the prosecution case. First, the admitted delay in notifying Jones. Two, the failure to bring to the stand any member of the Jones household who would confirm that Jones had been notified and had policemen guarding him night and day. Three, if there was a policeman in the house, why was he removed on the day Kerrigan arrived? The behavior of Jones -- going off to work alone and working in his backyard -- suggests he was not aware of the danger. The behavior of Kerrigan, who was supposedly as smart as a whip, and yet whose behavior insured he would be caught. And, finally, the behavior of McParland, who made no effort to warn Jones, even as the gunmen arrived in his neighborhood and who sat in Carroll's saloon in Tamaqua drinking with his brothers on the night before Jones was killed.

All of the above would suggest that the Pinkertons, Franklin Gowen, Charles Parrish, Asa Packer, William Zehner, the Coal and Iron Police, the Tamaqua Committee and James McParland were accessories to the killing of Jones because of their failure to protect him. And it is very obvious that this failure was deliberate -- that Jones died because they wanted him to die.

CHAPTER TWENTY-ONE

Some Questions About the Prosecution Case

Before going on to other aspects of McParland's testimony, there are a number of other elements of the prosecution case which leave a great many unanswered questions and which are worth taking a look at.

Let us return to one aspect of the prosecution case -- the Alec Campbell-McParland meeting in Mauch Chunk on August 9, a meeting mentioned briefly before.

This is a meeting that seemed to be of primary importance to the prosecution because McParland, Linden and Franklin dwelt on it at great length in their testimony. There are major discrepancies in the testimony and these are the discrepancies that once again the defense lawyers did not react to.

The basic elements of the story as presented by McParland, Franklin and Linden are as follows: Franklin said he was concerned about the murder of Yost and the plot to kill Jones, so he called a meeting with Linden and McParland and they met in Mauch Chunk on August 9. After they completed their meeting, they were walking down the street and bumped into Alec Campbell, Hugh McGeehan and a man named Phillips.

McParland left Franklin and Linden and joined Alec Campbell, and Alec Campbell told him he was in Mauch Chunk to help McGeehan get a liquor license. Campbell said he was helping McGeehan because of the "fine job" McGeehan did in murdering Yost.

Later Campbell, McGeehan and McParland took the train back to Lansford, and Linden also boarded the train and sat near the trio and was able to hear them talk together.

Now the reason the prosecution would focus on this meeting is obvious: it showed Alec Campbell "rewarding" Hugh McGeehan for killing Yost; it enabled McParland, Franklin and Gowan to swear that they saw McGeehan and Campbell together in Mauch Chunk; and it collaborated other prosecution evidence that Campbell and McGeehan were in fact at the court house in Mauch Chunk on August 9 and did apply for a liquor license for McGeehan.

However, the account of the event was presented with such theatrical intensity, and the prosecution went out of its way to present the meeting as occurring by pure chance, that an objective observer would come to the conclusion that there is something about this tale that just does not add up -- that even if lies were not being told by prosecution witnesses, that the whole truth was not being told either. A cross-referencing of the testimony of Linden, McParland and Franklin unearths many discrepancies in the tale and these discrepancies suggest that the meeting did not happen by chance if it happened at all, but was planned carefully by the Pinkertons.

The fact that the meeting did not occur by chance is easily determined by the evidence McParland presented earlier about his meetings with Alec Campbell on July 15, 18, and August 4. McParland in this earlier testimony touched on the fact that Campbell was going to help McGeehan get a tavern license and given this it would have been obvious that Campbell would have to go to the county court house at Mauch Chunk to help McGeehan get the license. A simple question by McParland to Campbell would have determined which day the appointment in the court house was set for, and then it would have been easy to get Linden and Franklin to rendezvous in Mauch Chunk so that they could say they saw Campbell and McGeehan together. Chance or coincidence had nothing to do with it.

However, this focuses on another more critical issue: it suggests that the Pinkertons were already building a case against Alec Campbell on August 9 for the murder of John P. Jones, while Jones was still alive and walking around the streets of Lansford. He would not die for another four weeks, until September 3.

No wonder then, the prosecution had gone to such lengths to portray the meeting as accidental. To do otherwise would imply that they were gathering evidence to use against Campbell for the murder of Jones, prior to Jones' being murdered.

There was other testimony introduced by the prosecution to collaborate the prosecution's contention that Campbell rewarded McGeehan for the murder of Yost that should have weakened the prosecution case if the defense had taken advantage of the opportunities offered it.

For instance, the prosecution introduced documents which indicated that Campbell had co-signed for the McGeehan license and the McGeehan lease on his saloon at Summit Hill.

But the lease document also revealed that the saloon was nothing more than the basement of a two-family house, and the rent was only $8 per month, and, when one considers that a miner at this time made $60-$70 per month, the $8 per month rent was very small, only a few day's wages.

121

Yet, the prosecution told the jury that Alec Campbell had set up McGeehan in a saloon, as if some considerable fortune had been spent on the project, whereas in reality, according to the prosecution witnesses, the place was a cellar and the rent was only a pittance.

It must be noted also that Campbell was a liquor wholesaler and distributor and the more liquor he could sell to saloons the more profit he would make so it was in his financial interest to co-sign a lease with McGeehan, because McGeehan would then buy all his liquor from him.

The defense lawyers made no attempt to argue that this was not a case of a godfather rewarding a young criminal, but rather an ordinary business transaction, which Campbell had entered into on other occasions -- also with Welshmen, helping them set up saloons -- and instead let the prosecution have a free hand at claiming Campbell had rewarded McGeehan.

Now, let us go back to the McParland, Linden, Franklin testimony on that meeting in Mauch Chunk and examine how each described the event and what the discrepancies were in their testimony.

First, McParland. According to McParland he had gone to Mauch Chunk to meet Franklin and Linden and after the discussion he and Linden had walked down Broadway and both saw Alec Campbell, Hugh McGeehan and Barney Phillips, county recorder, standing outside the court house. McParland, who was on the other side of the street, left Linden and went over and joined Campbell and McGeehan and all three went into Ambrosher's saloon for a drink. Campbell asked McParland whom he had been with and McParland replied that it was only a drunk he had met. Then Campbell, McGeehan and McParland took the switchback train to Summit Hill, and Linden came on the train with them, and sat nearby. McParland said he talked in a loud voice to Campbell and McGeehan, mentioning their names so Linden would know who they were. Campbell, McParland and McGeehan got off at Summit Hill and McParland walked a mile down the hill with Campbell to Campbell's hotel at Lansford, where he spent the night.

Now we have Linden's account of the meeting. Linden said that Franklin called them to a meeting at Mauch Chunk in order to discuss the possibility of putting another undercover detective on the scene to help head off the murder of Jones.

Linden said he met McParland in front of the Mansion House and had a discussion and then both went to the American Hotel for a drink and some more discussions. After that they left the hotel and walked down the street, where they saw a group of seven standing in front of the court house. He said Alec Campbell and McGeehan were among them and that he recognized both Campbell and McGeehan from prior descriptions given to him by McParland. He said that he was very much afraid that he would have been recognized as a policeman and that McParland's cover would have been blown because he was seen in his company, so he walked quickly away and later met with Franklin. Later still, he took the train to Summit Hill, along with Campbell, McGeehan, Phillips and McParland, and got off at Summit Hill to explore that area and also the Lansford area in order to determine the type of terrain the new detective was going to be working in.

The Linden testimony differs from the McParland testimony on several points. McParland said he, Franklin and Linden had met and had their discussion, and that Linden and McParland had met Alec Campbell after the Franklin meeting.

Linden, however, said he and McParland met first, and that they had met Alec Campbell before they had a chance to meet with Franklin, and that he met Franklin without McParland.

Linden said he recognized Alec Campbell and McGeehan from prior descriptions given by McParland; McParland said that Linden did not know them and that he had talked loudly in the train to Summit Hill in order to identify them.

Linden said there were seven people in front of the court house; McParland said there were three.

Linden said he was afraid that McParland's cover was blown because he was seen in his presence -- yet he boarded the train to Summit Hill with them and sat nearby. Linden talked about putting another detective on the job; McParland does not mention it.

Next up is Benjamin Franklin, who had called for the meeting at Mauch Chunk. This is Franklin's version.

Franklin said he called the meeting in order to determine if it would be a good idea to put another detective on the job at Summit Hill to keep an eye on McGeehan. He said he brought this detective (whom he did not identify) with him from Philadelphia to Mauch Chunk and he, the detective, McParland and Linden met in front of the Mansion House for a discussion.

Later, he said he took the train to Summit Hill to look the place over, and that the whole purpose of his involvement in Mauch Chunk and Summit Hill was to keep an eye on McGeehan in order to prevent the murder of Jones.

123

In this testimony, we have Allan Pinkerton's right-hand man, who is the boss of the Philadelphia office and the superintendent to whom both Linden and McParland report, say that on that day, August 9, he wanted a detective to go to Summit Hill to keep an eye on Hugh McGeehan in order to prevent the murder of Jones.

This is the same Franklin who testified hours earlier that McParland had sent him a report that the plot against Jones was being carried out by Alec Campbell with the help of James Kerrigan and that the murder was to take place near the Jones home in Lansford.

Why put a detective to watch McGeehan, who according to McParland was not going to be involved in the Jones killing, and why put him in Summit Hill when the killing was going to take place a mile and a half away at Lansford? And where did Alec Campbell come into this, because Franklin's testimony suggested McGeehan was the prime mover?

Also, Franklin's testimony was in conflict with both McParland's and Linden's over who met whom where and what happened afterwards.

All of this raises the possibility that there was no Pinkerton summit in Mauch Chunk at all on August 9 and that the idea of the meeting was just invented so that Linden, Franklin and McParland could testify that they saw Campbell and McGeehan there at the court house, and to dramatize that meeting for the jury.

If there had been a meeting, all of the participants would be in agreement on what had occurred, or at least agree on major points. But here each of the Pinkertons tells a different story, so obviously the only conclusion I could come to is that they had been telling lies, and doing so in order to make a case against Alec Campbell.

The Pinkertons and the prosecution had made a great deal of fuss about this meeting. Allan Pinkerton in his book treated it as a major dramatic event. Perhaps they did so because it provided an important piece of strategy in their plan to put a noose around the neck of Alec Campbell. It is amazing, however, how incompetent they were in their presentation, contradicting each other at every turn. It is even more amazing how Campbell's lawyers let them get away with it.

* * * *

There were several other segments of the trial which were puzzling, simply because both the defense and the prosecution went back and forth for hours over issues whose importance was not clear, and it must have

124

been very confusing for the jury, because it is still confusing to anyone who reads the transcript.

One of these issues was how James McParland suddenly went bald and what he did about this baldness.

The issue comes up when the prosecution accused Alec Campbell of trying to recruit witnesses to swear false testimony at the trial of James Kerrigan. The Kerrigan trial never took place because Kerrigan turned state's evidence.

Two of these witnesses, William McCauley and John McShea, whom McParland had accused in his testimony of being the witnesses recruited by Campbell, came on the stand at the request of the prosecution.

According to McParland he had, when he was still posing as McKenna, personally gone to Anderoid to get these two men to swear that Kerrigan was at a wake in Anderoid the night before the Jones killing and that they were with him. McParland said Campbell had sent him to Anderoid to recruit the witnesses.

However, William McCauley said he did not know Kerrigan, had never met Alec Campbell and while he had met a man that night who tried to get him to swear false testimony, he did not think it was McParland alias McKenna, "That man was sickly looking, kind of delicate. He did not look like a working man. I don't think it was him," pointing at James McParland.

John McShea also said he had been approached by a man named Jim McKenna, but that he did not look at all "like that man," pointing to McParland. "I do not recognize him at all," he said.

The testimony of these two raises an interesting question. Was it one of the other two McParland brothers who was up in Anderoid recruiting witnesses? Or was it one of the other McParland brothers who was posing as James McParland on the witness stand?

That issue never came up, of course, because neither of these two witnesses, or the defense, or few other people, were aware that there was more than one McParland in the coal regions, and so McShea and McCauley just said that the James McKenna they saw in Anderoid did not look like the James McKenna/James McParland they saw in the court and they did not know the reason for this and did not make a great fuss about it.

But Linden, Franklin and McParland must have seen the red lights go up and they were back on the witness stand to tell how McParland had lost all his hair suddenly in 1875 and had taken to wearing a wig.

Each of them spent a long time on the witness stand on this issue and the defense questioned them endlessly about it, but unless an observer were to know that there was more than one McParland in the coal fields the whole issue of his baldness would seem totally irrelevant and of minor importance.

One wonders what the jury thought of these hours of testimony and there must have been a great deal of confusion about what the issue was all about, since neither the defense or the prosecution indicated that there was a serious question about the identity of the James McParland who was a witness for the prosecution or the James McParland who had been running around posing as tough Molly Maguire James McKenna. It only made sense if one knew of the existence of Charles and Edward McParland -- and this is why the Pinkertons got so spooked up about the McShea and McCauley testimony.

But the questioning trailed off and the media of the era must have been confused by the testimony also, because they paid no attention to it, and it was simply transcribed and became part of the official record, destined to generate no speculation about its meaning.

The second issue that generated a great deal of testimony without the reason for the testimony being obvious was the $5 note found on James Kerrigan when he was arrested with Kelly and Doyle.

The defense lawyers asked endless questions of Wallace Guss, who arrested Kerrigan, about the $5. They asked where Guss had found it on Kerrigan, why he did not take it from Kerrigan, and what Kerrigan had done with it afterwards.

The $5 issue first came up when Kerrigan stated that Alec Campbell had given him $5 on the morning of the killing and that he was to use the $5 to buy whiskey for the men after the murder of Jones.

Kerrigan said he got the whiskey in Tamaqua, but the saloon owner did not have change for $5, so he still had the $5 on him when he was arrested.

The prosecution and the defense went back and forth with Wallace Guss a great deal about this $5 without spelling out the significance of the testimony.

Perhaps the explanation is that the prosecution believed that Kerrigan's testimony that he had received $5 from Campbell was important, because it indicated Campbell was rewarding killers, and therefore it was important to show he had $5 on him.

But Kerrigan also testified he had bought whiskey after the killing, so the defense was asking how you can have $5 if you spent it. And the prosecution said he did not spend it because the bar had no change.

There was no resolution to this issue and the conflicting testimony, like a great deal of other such testimony, remains a puzzling sidebar to the main themes of the trial. After that, the prosecution rested its case.

CHAPTER TWENTY-TWO

The Defense Testimony

The defense strategy was to bring on a series of witnesses who contradicted the testimony given by Kerrigan and McParland.

Kerrigan had said that he had brought Doyle and Kelly to Alec Campbell's bar at 9:00 p.m. on September 1. Patrick McNeilus said he was in Alec Campbell's bar all evening on September 1 and that John Boyle and Hugh Dugan were with him there, and that Doyle, Kelly or Kerrigan did not come into the tavern. He said Alec Campbell was there all night. He said the only person to come in all night was Michael Carr.

Hugh Dugan was the next witness and he agreed with everything McNeilus had said.

Michael Carr was up next and he said Boyle, Dugan, McNeilus and Campbell were in the bar when he came in and he stayed until closing. He said Doyle, Kelly and Kerrigan did not come into the bar.

Ellen Breslin, the sister-in-law of Alec Campbell who worked as a maid in the hotel, said that Kerrigan, Kelly or Doyle did not come into the hotel on either the first or second. She said that Kerrigan lied when he said the trio slept in the bar on the second, because she helped lock up and there was no one in the tavern.

Peter Shovelin said he came into Alec Campbell's bar on September 2, the night before the murder, at 9:00 p.m. and the only persons in the place were James Condon and John Gotlec. He said he helped close the place and Kerrigan, Doyle and Kelly were not there. He also said he was in Hugh McGeehan's bar in Summit Hill between 8:00 p.m. and 11:00 p.m. on the first and that Alec Campbell, Kerrigan, Doyle and Kelly did not enter the place.

The prosecution attorneys cross-examined Shovelin at length but could not shake his story, as he was very forceful and good under pressure.

Daniel Malloy, who was a boarder at Alec Campbell's, said he did not see Kerrigan Doyle or Kelly around the house on either the first or the second, and that, in spite of Kerrigan's testimony that Doyle and Kelly had dinner upstairs on the second, that he was the only one -- except the Campbell family -- who had dinner that night.

John Dugan said he was in McGeehan's bottling porter on September 2, between 2:00 p.m. and 6:30 p.m. when Kerrigan said he was there, and Dugan said he did not see Kerrigan.

Squire Jacob Lutz, justice of the peace, said Kerrigan lied when he said that he met him in Carrol's in Tamaqua, just as Kerrigan was leaving Carrol's to go to Alec Campbell's at Lansford. He said Kerrigan was not in Carrol's that night. Lutz also said the chief burgess of Tamaqua and members of the Tamaqua Council had pressured him not to be a defense witness for Campbell.

Mrs. Rose Breslin, mother-in-law of Alec Campbell, said Kerrigan, Doyle and Kelly were not around the house on either the first or the second.

Pat McNeilus said that McParland was a troublemaker who was vicious and violent.

John McGinley, who kept a saloon and hotel in Mauch Chunk, said McParland was a hopeless drunk who seemed to have an endless supply of money. He said he threw him out of the saloon twice for being obnoxious.

John McShea said there was no such organization as the Molly Maguires and that the AOH was a respectable fraternal organization. He said any violence that came about happened because of McParland.

James Condon said he was in Alec Campbell's at 6:00 a.m. on the third, one hour before the Jones murder. He said he did not see Kerrigan, Doyle or Kelly there, and they did not leave the place at 7:00 p.m. to kill Jones. He said both of Jones' sisters, Mrs. Fox and Mrs. James, saw him outside the tavern at 7:15 p.m., when word of the Jones killing got out.

Condon says he was threatened by the police and mine boss Churchill and told not to be a defense witness, but he wanted to tell the truth.

Samuel Allen, a Welshman, said he had known Alec Campbell since he came from Ireland and had never known him to cause trouble.

William Simmons, a newspaper reporter, said Alec Campbell was highly respected in the community and he had never heard anybody say anything about him until he was arrested.

Dr. James Donahue said the Campbells were respectable and very popular in the community.

John Slattery said McParland was a coward and a drunk and he once boasted he would send a dozen members of the AOH to the gallows.

John Gallagher said he had been a business partner of Campbell's for eight years and always found him honest and reliable.

Nancie Gallagher said Campbell was very influential in both Carbon and Schuylkill counties and was sought after by politicians when they were running for office.

Fred Breneiser and Jacob Chintman said they had heard nothing against Campbell and had never heard of him being a Molly Maguire until his arrest.

Casper Bull said he lived near Campbell for five years and had never heard him called a leader of the Molly Maguires or had heard anything against him.

Adam Hartwig said he knew Campbell for five years and never heard a bad word about him.

Daniel Shepp of the Tamaqua Committee admitted that all of the bad reputation Campbell had acquired had come from the McParland report of July 17, and from no other source. But he said he believed McParland.

The defense rested.

CHAPTER TWENTY-THREE

The Ultimate Question About Alec Campbell. Guilty or Innocent?

After the prosecution and the defense had presented their case, the trial was over except for final arguments presented by both sides and the judge's instruction to the jury. At this point I had heard all of the evidence presented by both sides and it was time for me to make an analysis of what I had read.

I knew, of course, the verdict of the jury, and I knew the consequences of that verdict, but it was time now for me to act as judge and jury and come to my own conclusions about Alec Campbell's guilt or innocence based on the evidence.

First, I went over all the notes I had taken during my analysis of the prosecution case, and after some thought I came to the following conclusion.

The prosecution had presented credible evidence that James Kerrigan, Edward Kelly and Michael Doyle had been in Lansford for two days prior to the Jones murder and all the evidence suggested that they had in fact killed Jones and then fled to Tamaqua, where they were arrested.

Did I have any doubt about this? I had none whatsoever -- there was a whole array of witnesses and it was out of the question that all of them were lying.

So, Kerrigan, Doyle and Kelly had killed Jones, and I was absolutely sure that the evidence against them was watertight and could not be disputed.

The next question -- the vital question as far as I was concerned -- was what role Alec Campbell played in this murder, and whether the prosecution had proved beyond a shadow of a doubt that he was, as charged, an accessory before the fact.

The prosecution case rested solely on the testimony of two witnesses: James Kerrigan and James McParland, because it was they and they alone who had tied him into the Jones murder.

How credible was James Kerrigan's evidence? What would a really impartial observer think of this evidence as it was presented in court? I read the Kerrigan testimony one more time and I came to the conclusion that it was so full of holes, so full of contradictions and so lacking in credibility that I did not believe that I would have convicted anyone based on what he said, and therefore I would have dismissed all of his testimony as worthless.

What about McParland? How did he come across? One more reading of McParland's testimony showed that McParland was a very credible witness -- cool, unflappable, he projected sincerity, and generally came across as an honest professional. However, McParland had proved during his years undercover that he was a talented actor, and, given the fact that I knew he was lying on critical issues, I came to the conclusion that his behavior on the stand was another good performance, presented with all the expertise of a theatrical genius.

McParland's worst enemies were his allies -- his two Pinkerton bosses, Linden and Franklin, who contradicted his testimony at every turn. His enemies also were the members of the Tamaqua Committee -- Shepp, Guss and the Beards, who could not get a story straight either.

McParland never contradicted himself, and he was always alert and able to give the same tale no matter how many times he was questioned, and it was only when his evidence was compared to the evidence of some of his colleagues on the same subject that this testimony became open to question. As stand-alone evidence, however, it was remarkably sound.

Should Alec Campbell have been convicted on the evidence of James McParland? This was a complex question. The jury was not aware that McParland had two brothers in the area and therefore had ample opportunity to warn Jones and save his live. The jury was not briefed by Campbell's lawyers that most of McParland's evidence was contradicted by other prosecution witnesses, and unless they were exceptionally alert and were taking notes the contradictions could possibly have escaped some of them. However, it would be hard to see how even a jury that was half asleep could have failed to note that the Pinkertons had received a warning on July 19 that Jones was going to be killed and did not notify anyone until August 5.

Should Campbell have been convicted on McParland's evidence -- this was the basic question for me and it was the one which had taken me 15 years to confront. My answer is no -- he should not have been convicted, simply because McParland's evidence was not supported by a credible witness, and he was contradicted by his own allies. Alec Campbell should never have been given a guilty verdict based on the McParland evidence presented at his trial.

But I realized that, as soon as I had answered that basic question, there was a question that was even more basic and that was the question of whether or not Alec Campbell was innocent of all the charges brought against him. And I did not mean innocent in the legal sense alone -- I was far more interested in the question of whether or not he was really and truly innocent.

This was a very difficult question and I realized, of course, that it probably was an impossible one to answer. However, I decided to give it a try and I went over both the prosecution evidence and the defense evidence one more time to see if I could come to some conclusion.

I had made some basic decisions earlier about the validity of part of the prosecution case, and I had also come up with a theory about how and why the Jones killing was set up, and so I decided to analyze Alec Campbell's defense testimony given my theory and my conviction that the 60 prosecution witnesses in phase one were telling the truth.

If my theory was correct -- that Kerrigan had been blackmailed into the Jones killing because the Pinkertons had discovered his involvement in the Yost killing -- then there would have been no doubt that Kerrigan would have come to Alec Campbell's hotel on September 1, as he swore he did, because involving AOH leader Alec Campbell was the reason for killing Jones in the first place. And there would be no doubt that Kerrigan, Doyle and Kelly would also have visited Hugh McGeehan's saloon, because involving union agitator McGeehan was also very much part of the plan. And all the witnesses who saw the trio did so because it was part of the plan for the trio to be seen, and Kerrigan insured this would happen.

Where did this leave those defense witnesses who swore that Kerrigan, Kelly and Doyle had never come into either Campbell's hotel or McGeehan's saloon on September 1, 2, and 3? If my theory was correct, then all of them had lied, and Alec Campbell knew they lied, because he must have met the trio on the dates in question, in spite of what his sister-in-law, his mother-in-law, and his friends had sworn.

If Alec Campbell were completely innocent of any involvement in the Jones killing, why would he get witnesses to lie -- to say Kerrigan, Doyle and Kelly were not on his premises on these critical dates?

The answer to that might be that after Kerrigan, Kelly and Doyle were arrested, he realized his vulnerability and tried to defend himself by claiming that the trio had not been at his place, and he did so without realizing that the prosecution had lined up scores of credible witnesses, some of whom placed the trio on the street outside his house.

Would an innocent man lie like that, or would he just say that Kerrigan, Kelly and Doyle were in his hotel but that he had not idea what they were up to? I did not know the answer to this question, and I did not know whose idea it was to get the witnesses to lie -- whether it was Alec Campbell's or those defense lawyers who already had put a noose around Campbell's neck because of their incompetence.

What were the possibilities anyway as far as Campbell's guilt or innocence was concerned? I made a list of them.

1. He was completely innocent and was the victim of a frame-up.
2. He had no part in the planning or execution of the murder, but he suspected Kerrigan was up to no good when he arrived in his bar and made no effort to stop him.
3. Kerrigan told him of the plan to kill Jones, and Campbell not only made no effort to stop him, but gave him moral support.
4. Campbell hated Jones and the Pinkertons played on this by getting McParland and Kerrigan to propose the murder, which Campbell agreed to.
5. Campbell hated Jones and asked McParland to help him kill the mine boss, and McParland blackmailed Kerrigan into getting involved so that Campbell and McGeehan could be set up to be convicted for the murder.

Which of these possibilities would have fitted in with my theory? The answer was that any one of them would, either Campbell's total innocence or Campbell's heavy involvement, and I had no credible evidence which would enable me to come to a decision on any of these possibilities.

Therefore, I could only conclude that from a legal point of view Alec Campbell was not guilty of the charges brought against him, and as far as the ultimate question of his innocence was concerned, only God and Alec Campbell knew the answer to that question.

CHAPTER TWENTY-FOUR

A Death Sentence

The Campbell lawyers had failed to promote Campbell's interests during the trial, but when the testimony had been presented by both the prosecution and the defense and it was time for summation, both Kalbfus and Fox were eloquent in their defense of Campbell and in their denunciation of both McParland and Kerrigan. They then displayed all the vigor and intelligence that should have been directed at destroying the prosecution witnesses, such as Kerrigan, McParland, Linden, Guss, Shepp, Baird, Zehner and Franklin, who could have been annihilated by a law student.

It was too late at this stage of the trial to come awake, and one wonders if these closing remarks were really a strategy to quell any accusation that they did not do their best to protect Alec Campbell.

Kalbfus was up first and he told the jury that the only reason the prosecution wanted to hang Campbell was because he was a leader of the AOH in Carbon County.

"I look into the books for the admissibility of James Kerrigan's evidence, under the head of infamy. Under Kerrigan's authority Campbell is to die and his wife made a widow. Kerrigan is the confessed accomplice of the killing of Yost; he is the captain of the men who killed Jones. He has no soul; he is a wreck of total depravity.

"He killed Jones and now he wants to kill Campbell. Gentlemen of the jury, do you mean to say that Kerrigan, who has already killed a man, would hesitate a moment to go upon that witness stand and swear falsely to save his own life."

Then Kalbfus went after McParland. "Who is this man McParland? What inspired Brutus to slay Caesar? Why did Booth kill Lincoln? The one answer will do for both questions and that is -- ambition.

"He is a teamster, a half-made chemist and a whiskey dealer. He said he killed a man in Buffalo. You heard him say so. He said he was a counterfeiter and was living on counterfeit gains. Under oath he told these things and said he lied. He told Campbell he had shot a man in Tamaqua. He is the man who incited the burning of the Catawissa Bridge, as testified to by a witness who has not been contradicted. He is a hireling of the

Reading Railroad Company. The AOH was an honorable organization until McParland and Kerrigan disgraced it.

"Who is McParland? He is the man who wrote Franklin and told him John P. Jones was to be killed. Blast him. He was only four miles from the killing of Jones and he would not save his life.

"I would call him a liar. Coward! He abetted, he planned, he connived the killing of John P. Jones, and you know it.

"He was the man who fixed the rewards for the killing that was done and he was the brains of the society. I say that the only evidence against Alec Campbell is McParland's and you are to disbelieve it utterly."

Kalbfus talked for two hours, lambasting both star witnesses, but evidently making no impression on the Welsh and German jury who listened to him. They may have already made up their minds, possibly even before the trial began.

Attorney Fox also came after McParland, and he concentrated his fire on McParland's role as an informer.

"The detectives or informers of Ireland are nothing less than the heresy of English courts. I say a man who enters a conspiracy and encourages men to commit crime is just as guilty as those who commit the crime. A man who employs a systematic mode of lying in order to gain a desirable end is a detestable man.

"It may be necessary in human society that men should enter the bands of criminals to detect crime. But that man's motive should be good alone, and he should not be a conspirator in and an encourager of crime. Now, take McParland upon his own story he encouraged and promulgated the murder of Jones. McParland is the man who made Mrs. Jones a widow.

"Where is the principle in that if a man informs the police of a murder and afterwards takes part in the affair, that he is not part of the murder? There is no such thing in the world."

Judge Dreher was up next, and in charging the jury, Dreher went over many points of law and emphasized that Alec Campbell could be found guilty of murder in the first degree if the jury thought he was an accessory before the fact in the killing of Jones.

Then he made two very important points -- the first: "James Kerrigan is an acknowledged accomplice in the murder of Jones. He is therefore an infamous witness and we charge you not to convict the prisoner on the uncorroborated evidence of this man."

The second: "James McParland is a man of good character and therefore not an infamous witness and his evidence should be treated by you with as much weight as that of other witnesses."

When the jury brought in a verdict later that day, it was pronounced by foreman of the jury, William F. Roberts, as "Guilty of murder in the first degree."

When the verdict was read, Mrs. Alec Campbell burst into tears and so did Sarah and Annie Campbell. Alec and his brother James comforted them.

Then Mrs. Campbell turned on McParland, who had been sitting on the other side of the room and called him a "dirty little killer." She also said that Gowen and McParland were "not going to get away with this."

As Alec Campbell was being led back to jail, he said, "Don't worry. It will be all right."

Kalbfus immediately asked that Campbell be granted a new trial and he presented seven reasons:

1. The verdict is against the weight of the evidence.
2. The court erred in admitting evidence tending to show that the defendant was an accessory before the fact to the killing of John P. Jones, by a pistol shot fired by Michael J. Doyle or Michael Kelly in the absence of defendant.
3. The evidence showed James Kerrigan was an accomplice in the murder and as he was not corroborated in material points the jury ought to have acquitted the defendant.
4. James Kerrigan went upon the witness stand as an infamous witness, tainted with suspicion, and as he was contradicted in material points by the testimony of credible witnesses, the jury ought to have acquitted the defendant.
5. The evidence of James McParland showed he was an accessory before the fact, and as he was not corroborated in material points, the jury ought to have acquitted the defendant.
6. The testimony of McParland, having been contradicted in material points by the evidence of credible witnesses, the jury ought to have acquitted the defendant.
7. The court erred in the exercise of their discretion in permitting James Kerrigan to have testified against the defendant.

Kalbfus knew there was no possibility of the petition being taking seriously. The judge who would review the petition, Judge Dreher, was the one who let Kerrigan testify, and he was the judge who said in his summation that McParland was an honest man and not an accessory to the Jones murder. So, there was no chance Dreher was going to reverse himself, and the Kalbfus petition for a new trial was a mere formality that gave the Campbells the idea that there was still hope.

Dreher accepted the petition and said he would hear arguments on July 24.

He heard these arguments in the presence of the Campbells on July 24 and then reserved decision until August 28.

At 2:00 p.m. on Monday, August 28, the Campbell family, the defense and prosecution attorneys, as well as a capacity audience of spectators, including the Jones family, Pinkerton agents, Linden and Franklin, General Albright, Charles Parrish, Asa Packer, and James McParland.

Dreher went over each point in the defense motion in turn and dismissed every one of them, and he then denied the defendant a new trial.

Alec Campbell listened to all of this with the self-control that he had exhibited throughout his trial.

Campbell was called before the bench by Dreher, and the judge said the following to him:

"This is most unpleasant, this duty I must perform. I deeply commiserate with you and your wife in the unfortunate position in which you are placed. But I also remember the tears of the bereaved wife and orphans of John P. Jones. Yet no feeling for either the dead or living must swerve us from the path of duty. The law of God and men must be observed. I refrain from further comment and ask you, Alexander Campbell, have you aught to say, why the judgement of the law of Pennsylvania should not be pronounced."

Campbell replied, "Only this judge. I am innocent of this crime before God, but I am willing to suffer for the guilty. There is too much prejudice in these courts for me to get a fair trial."

Campbell's comment about being "willing to suffer for the guilty" must be viewed within the context of the period and Campbell's Catholic faith: it was believed by Irish Catholics of that time that those who were "crucified" or executed when they were innocent stood an excellent chance of going to Heaven.

Dreher ignored Campbell's comment and then pronounced the death sentence.

138

"You are yet a young man. Up to the time when you were arrested for this crime you were associated in toil with the men who a jury of the citizens of this county have said are guilty. You abetted them and advised them in the homicide and have been found guilty as a principal in the crime.

"To me, this is a most fearful task, but I have nothing more to say but this: that the sentence of the court is that you, Alec Campbell, be taken from hence to the county jail, and from there to the place of execution, and that you be hanged by the neck until you are dead, and may God in his infinite goodness have mercy on your soul."

Dreher's claim that this was an "unpleasant duty" and a "fearful task" was listened to with grim humor by many of those present. Dreher had been brought into Carbon County for these trials because he was known as a hanging judge who not only handed out death sentences, but never missed an execution. He was there when Alec Campbell was hanged.

The sentence was greeted with applause by the Jones family and with tears by the Campbell family. The prosecution attorneys crowded around the judge and shook his hand.

Campbell turned to the newsmen and repeated his claim of innocence and asked God to be his witness. Mrs. Campbell said her husband had never done anything wrong.

Then the sheriff led Campbell away.

CHAPTER TWENTY-FIVE

Another Murder Conviction

Campbell's trial, conviction and death sentence were followed by scores of other trials all over the anthracite region, with most of the leaders of the Irish community being indicted on capital offenses.

None of the leaders, except Jack Kehoe, chief of police of Girardville, were accused of committing the murders themselves, but were instead indicted as accessories.

All of McParland's close associates, who were his friends when he was posing as James McKenna, were allowed to fade away into oblivion, even though some of these, like Frank McAndrews, were like McParland either involved in the planning of the murders of Sanger, Uren, Jones and James, or actually had committed them.

McParland's two brothers, Edward and Charles, also faded away, and more than ninety-nine percent of the residents of Carbon and Schuylkill counties had not even been aware of their presence.

There were those living in the area who did know, however, like the Schoepple family of Pottsville, who would not let their daughter Emily marry Charles McParland. So did the Lynch family, also of Schuylkill County, who did let their daughter marry Charles McParland. But neither of these families told anyone, or came forward with the evidence that might have saved Alec Campbell or some of the other condemned Mollies.

Franklin Gowen strutted around the region boasting he was going to hang every Mollie that was locked up and he took a very active part in the prosecution at many of the trials. Asa Packer and Charles Parrish, however, continued to remain in the background.

A glutton for publicity, Gowen handled most of the final speeches to the juries, knowing every word would be reported in newspapers across the country.

The fact that a company president who had everything to gain by destroying the union and the AOH would be allowed to conduct the prosecutions and have his own lawyers as his assistants tells us something about how the judicial system worked in Pennsylvania in 1876.

However, Gowen, Packer, and Parrish were aware of the weakness of the prosecution case against Campbell, and, no doubt, also aware of the many discrepancies that would have got the case thrown out of court had they not the judge and the jury in their hip pocket and the defense lawyers asleep.

They were mainly afraid of the appeal to the Supreme Court which Mrs. Alec Campbell had insisted upon because, even though Gowen, Packer and Parrish had many allies on the Supreme Court, they had a few enemies also, and they did not want Campbell to escape the noose. So, they had Campbell indicted for the murder of Morgan Powell, who had been killed in 1871.

Two men had been arrested at the time of the Powell murder, but had been acquitted for lack of evidence. During that trial there had been no suggestion that Alec Campbell was involved, and no suggestion afterwards either, up to the time he was brought back into court and accused of the murder, along with three other men, none of whom had been mentioned in the first trial.

Indeed, local people who knew Powell thought he had been murdered by a Welshman named Llewellyn because Powell had been living for years with a woman who had been Llewellyn's wife, and whom Llewellyn had never divorced.

But Albright and District Attorney Siewers claimed Campbell had mine boss Powell killed because Powell would not give him a mine breast to work on, and instead gave the mine breasts to newcomers from Wales.

Gowen, Packer, Parrish and Albright really wanted another death sentence as insurance, in case Campbell was acquitted on appeal on the Jones killing and this was the reason he was indicted for the murder of Powell.

Campbell went to trial on these charges in December of 1876, represented again by Kalbfus, and as a number of death sentences had already been handed out to other defendants in the Powell case, the prosecution had no trouble in intimidating men they had convicted in the Powell case into turning state's evidence. These men, as well as James Kerrigan, swore Campbell hated Powell because he would not give him a mine breast and that he had wanted Powell dead.

In addition, Powell's young daughter swore that a man who looked like Campbell had come to their house the night before the murder and demanded that Powell give him a breast, and when Powell refused, the man had threatened her father.

The defense brought in only one witness, and the testimony of this witness should have been enough to destroy the prosecution case, because it destroyed all the motivation for Campbell's involvement, but it did not

141

work out that way and the hand-picked jury brought in another death sentence for Campbell.

The sole defense witness was Charles Powell, first cousin of Morgan Powell and the mine boss who was the direct supervisor of Alec Campbell when he worked in the mines.

Charles Powell said that Campbell had reported to him directly, not to Morgan Powell, who was the superintendent over several mines, including the one Charles Powell supervised.

Charles Powell said that there had been a great deal of trouble between Powell and the union -- the WBA -- over Welshmen always getting mine breasts and Irishmen getting very few. He said the president of the WBA, C. T. McHugh who had also been charged in the Powell murder, and who was now the principal witness against Campbell in exchange for immunity, had quarreled bitterly with his cousin over this issue, and so had a score of other miners.

But, he said Campbell had bought the right to work the breast from a Welsh miner 18 months before the murder and had worked it three months after the murder, when he sold it to his brother and went into the liquor distributing business.

Charles Powell said Campbell had never been a troublemaker or an instigator but he had stood up for his rights when he was a miner and had advised other miners to do the same. And he said Campbell had an excellent reputation until he was accused in the Jones killing.

Since the issue of Campbell's not being able to work the breast was the cornerstone of the prosecution case, Charles Powell's testimony should have been enough to acquit him, since there was no witness which put Campbell at the scene of the crime and no witness against him except McHugh and Charles Mulhearn, both of whom were infamous witnesses. But this did not happen and the judge handed down another death sentence, which was the insurance Gowen, Packer and Parrish wanted.

McParland and Kerrigan were also heavily involved in this trial, as both stated on the witness stand they had heard Alec Campbell talk about his involvement in the Powell case, and Robert Linden, McParland's Pinkerton supervisor, was also involved, admitting on the stand that he had first threatened McHugh and Mulhearn with the noose, and then promised them freedom if they cooperated. Linden also admitted giving money to the families of both McHugh and Mulhearn and taking care of them while they were in jail.

A curious sidebar to the case emerged in the Charles Powell testimony. Powell was being cross-examined by General Albright about the breast.

Albright: "Did Campbell tell you he could not get a breast from Morgan Powell?"
Powell: "No, he never told me of it."

At this point the cross-examination was interrupted by a completely different question and it is not clear who has asked the question.

Q: "What knowledge have you about Morgan Powell being married to a woman whose husband was still living?"
A: "I was told in 1855 that the woman in question married a man by the name of. . .I don't remember the name at the present time. I know the man by sight."
Q: "State whether he was reputed to be living and that the woman had another husband."

Powell went on to say that the woman had left her husband and got a job as a maid, and that when Morgan Powell came back from California, where he had been living, he had taken up with this woman, and married her.

The questioning then ended abruptly, leaving the impression that the woman had committed bigamy, and also the impression that the first husband may have been behind the Morgan Powell murder. The first husband's name was Samuel Llewellyn.

The subject was never brought up again and it is not clear who asked the question. But the question came when Charles Powell was telling General Albright that Alec Campbell had not complained about not getting a breast from Morgan Powell, so it was a timely interruption for the prosecution, because it changed the subject abruptly, even if it muddied the waters ever further.

It took less than a day to present the prosecution case, and the jury took less than an hour to hand down a verdict of guilty of murder in the first degree.

Alec Campbell was really and truly put in a corner and few would have given him any chance of escaping the hangman.

Campbell was sentenced to death again by Judge Dreher, who made

143

another sanctimonious speech about a "painful duty."

Campbell had become bitter by now as he realized the extent of the forces lined up against him, and he was especially bitter against C. T. McHugh, who had turned state's evidence in order to save his own neck. McHugh had been president of the Summit Hill chapter of the Workers Benevolent Association and a long time foe of Morgan Powell, but he had denied any animosity toward Powell, even though he had been indicted for his murder.

It is probable that McHugh had nothing to do with the killing either, but he was given the choice of the rope or freedom in exchange for testifying against Campbell and he took the offer of freedom.

Mrs. Alec Campbell and her two sisters-in-law Sarah and Annie screamed at McHugh in the courtroom and called him a coward and a liar. All three were evicted.

After the death sentence was pronounced, McHugh and Mulhearn were released and they vanished from the region and were never seen again.

James Kerrigan was also released and he, too, was not seen for years, although eventually he returned.

Alec Campbell was brought back to the Carbon County jail where he was incarcerated with three other men, all sentenced to death. Six more were over in the Pottsville jail under a death sentence and scores more had been given long prison sentences.

And there were those who had yet to be brought to trial, and many of these would also die on the gallows.

Gowen continued to boast to the media that he was going to hang all his enemies, but in spite of the death sentences, many of those sitting on death row just could not believe that the sentences would be carried out.

"They can't hang everybody," said James Roarity to a reporter.

But they could, and did, and James Roarity was one of ten to die in one day. Alec Campbell was another.

CHAPTER TWENTY-SIX

The Defense Appeals

The reality that his client Alec Campbell could end his life on the gallows seems to have galvanized Daniel Kalbfus into action in the days after the second death sentence was handed down.

From this point onwards Kalbfus would seem to have done everything possible to save Campbell from the gallows, but the question still remains why he ignored so many opportunities during the Jones trial to destroy the prosecution case. One wonders if the energy being displayed in early 1877 was belated recognition of the danger his client was in, or if it was a show put on by Kalbfus to project the image of a vigorous defense lawyer, when all along he knew that Campbell was on his way to the gallows.

Anyway Mrs. Alec Campbell and the other members of Campbell's family would not have allowed Kalbfus to leave any stone unturned, even if he wanted to sit back and let Alec Campbell die at the end of a rope, and they insisted that every avenue of appeal be explored.

First, Kalbfus appealed to the Pennsylvania Supreme Court, citing a total of 15 errors committed during Campbell's two trials, and asking that the verdicts be overturned.

But on March 27, the Honorable Daniel Agnew, chief justice of the Supreme Court, issued an affirmation of the judgment against Campbell and let the death sentence stand.

The next step was to petition the governor of Pennsylvania, John T. Handranft, for either a pardon or a commutation of the sentence to life. Alec Campbell would, at this stage, have settled for a life sentence, as it would have bought him time.

But Gowan, Packer, Parrish and Albright were determined not to allow Handranft to save Campbell's life, and so they started to tell the media that Campbell had helped Handranft get elected by raising funds for him and by making speeches in his support, and that Handranft planned to pay Campbell and the other Mollies back by pardoning them.

Their claims were partially true, of course. Alec Campbell had indeed helped Handranft defeat Gowen's hand-picked candidate for governor and he had helped raise funds. But the reason Handranft was uncomfortable about the death sentences had to do with the way the trials were conducted, and not because he wanted to save his supporters from the gallows.

However, the accusations against him put the governor on the spot. He told aides that he would be committing political suicide if he pardoned any condemned Molly and this fact was underscored by the uproar the accusations created in the Welsh and German communities in Carbon and Schuylkill counties.

When Kalbfus went to Harrisburg to present the petition to the governor personally, Mrs. Alec Campbell insisted on going along with him so that she too could plead for her husband's life.

Governor Handranft received the pair politely and listened carefully to what Kalbfus had to say. Mrs. Campbell was emotional and insisted her husband had not done anything wrong in his life and that he was being set up by Gowen because he had supported the union and had helped Gowen's political enemies get elected.

She then produced a testimonial that had just arrived from Alec Campbell's parents in Dungloe, County Donegal. It stated:

"We the undersigned beg to state that Alexander Campbell, at present of Summit Hill, America, but formerly of Dungloe, County Donegal, Ireland, conducted himself while at home dutifully, steadily and honestly; and that his parents are honest, industrious and respectable.
Dungloe, 6th March 77
Signed:
James Gallagher R.C. Adm. Dungloe, Co. Donegal.
William Hammond, Justice of the Peace, for Co. Donegal
Daniel O'Donnell, Parish Priest, Templecrone.
Michael Ward, C.C. Dungloe
Rev. William Jelb, A.B.T.C., Rector, Church of Ireland

Governor Handranft read the testimonial, and then said he was sorry -- that there was nothing he could do.

Mrs. Campbell said her husband was being murdered.

* * * *

But the governor, nevertheless, dragged his feet about signing the death warrant for Alec Campbell and the other condemned men. In order to keep the pressure on him, Asa Packer had E. R. Siewers, the Carbon County district attorney, send a letter to Handranft demanding that he sign the death warrant. Siewers wrote the letter and also handed a copy to the newspapers.

Mauch Chunk, Pa.
May 21, 1877

Hon. John T. Handranft
Governor of Pennsylvania

My Dear Sir:

In as much as the record of the Supreme Court in the case of Alexander Campbell and the Commonwealth has been certified to this County and the Remission has already been sent from the proper office of the County to your Excellency for final disposal of this matter -- I would beg leave to suggest if possible and practical the fixing of the death warrant for the Execution of Alexander Campbell as of the 21st of June A.D. 1877, the same day as that of Doyle and Kelly. Campbell was the prime mover in the assassination of John P. Jones and besides he was until his arrest most zealous of all in his endeavors to furnish perjured testimony if possible to acquit the men who perpetrated the deed of blood and thwart the ends of justice. In the view of expense and prolongation of any anticipated trouble from attempted rescue or otherwise, I think I only reiterate the wish of the people of this county and community that if possible the execution of Campbell may take place on the 21st of June.

Yours very respectfully,
E. R. Siewers

The allusion in the Siewers letter to "attempted rescue or otherwise" was part of a new publicity strategy that had been concocted by Gowen, Packer, Parrish and the Pinkertons.

The Pinkertons began to tell reporters that plans were afoot to rescue the Mollies both from Mauch Chunk jail and Pottsville jail and that thou-

147

sands of Mollies were up in the hills drilling for an insurrection.

Gowen was also talking to the media and telling them of the need to arm themselves, because sooner or later Pottsville and Mauch Chunk were going to be under siege.

In order to avoid all this, Packer and Gowen said they wanted the six Mollies in Pottsville jail and the four in Mauch Chunk jail sent to the gallows as soon as possible or else there would be a blood bath.

Handranft did not delay after receiving the Siewers letter and evaluating the mounting anti-Irish hullabaloo in the media. He may have thought his political life was at stake, and on the following day he signed Campbell's death warrant.

He sent the Campbell death warrant to the sheriff of Carbon County with the following note:

Executive Chamber
Harrisburg, May 22, 1877

Let death warrant issued to be executed upon the said <u>Alexander</u> <u>Campbell</u> on Thursday, the 21st day of June, A.D. 1877 between the hours of 10:00 a.m. and 3:00 p.m. by the sheriff of the county of Carbon in the manner by law directed.

G. Handranft
Governor

The governor received this reply from the sheriff's office, Mauch Chunk, on May 26, 1877

The Honorable John T. Handranft
Governor of Pennsylvania

My Dear Sir:

In persuance of the Death Warrant for the Execution of Alexander Campbell as received from you as of date of May 22, 1877, as within commanded, I read the said warrant (to Campbell) on the 24th day of May A.D. 1877 at 3 o'clock p.m. and filed the said warrant away for any further orders from your Excellency

148

Very Resply yours,
J. Raudenbush, Sheriff

When the Campbell family heard the door of the governor's mansion close on them, they had one last hope, and that was to petition the Board of Pardons.

Kalbfus wrote to the Board on June 2nd.

Dan'l Kalbfus
Attorney at Law
Office - opp. American Hotel
Manch Chunk, Pa. June 2nd 1877
To the Board of Pardons

Gentlemen:

I was one of the Counsel who defended Alex Campbell in his trial for the murder of John P. Jones. The character of the material witnesses against him, was so palpably infamous, and the game they played so certainly in the interests of their own forfeited necks, that I could not agree to a verdict that would take Campbell's life -- nor can I now.

I importune you gentlemen for commutation from death to imprisonment for life, and will feel that the public need has been advanced by this clemency.

Very truely,
Dan I. Kalbfus

The Board of Pardons hearing was held on June 16 and appeals were held not only for the life of Alec Campbell but for the lives of the nine other condemned men as well.

Campbell's wife Mary was present and so were his sisters Annie and Sarah, as well as attorney Daniel Kalbfus.

Kalbfus told the Board of Pardons that the verdict at his trial did not reflect an impartial review of the testimony, but rather was in response to "the clamor of the rabble."

He said he had never seen a situation like this or ever heard of such a situation, where whole segments of the population were being whipped up

149

into a blood lust by the media, and where even defense lawyers were abused. He said his client had not got a fair trial and was being railroaded to the gallows.

The appeal was denied, as were the appeals of the nine other men, and Mrs. Campbell wept as she finally confronted the reality that she would soon be a widow and that her little daughter Rose would be without a father.

When Campbell was told by his jailors that night of being turned down by the Board of Pardons, he took the news with the same strength he had displayed throughout the trial. He was completely calm.

"Well, I suppose I am facing the end. But if it is God's will, it is God's will, and I accept it. I am not the first innocent man to die on the gallows."

* * * *

Much as been written about the pressure Governor Handranft had been exposed to before he signed the death warrants and how it would have been "political suicide" for him not to sign them.

A couple of observations on that issue. First of all, any courageous and honorable man would not have signed anybody's death warrant if he had the kind of doubts that Handranft seemed to have had.

Secondly, Handranft not only signed the death warrants but he caved in under the demands of Packer, Gowen and Parrish that all of the ten men in the death cells be hanged on the same day, in a massive hanging orgy. Gowen, Packer and Parrish had wanted to teach the Irish union and political activists a bloody lesson in order to terrorize them, and the governor went along with it, and fixed all the executions for June 21, 1877.

Handranft did not have to do that. He could have fixed the executions weeks or months or days apart. Instead he went along with the execution carnival on the mine owners' insistence.

Handranft was either afraid of public opinion or the mine owners had something on him, and either way the governor was a man without courage or honor.

JAMES McPARLAN

JAMES KERRIGAN

FRANKLIN B. GOWEN

ALLAN PINKERTON

SARAH AND ANNIE CAMPBELL. 1885

ALEC CAMPBELL

JAMES AND MARY CAMPBELL, PATRICK CAMPBELL'S PARENTS.
1915. JAMES TOLD HIS FAMILY AND FRIENDS ALL ABOUT
HIS UNCLE ALEC.

PATRICK, EILEEN, PADRAIC AND NORA CAMPBELL. 1977.
THE MC PARLAND INVESTIGATION HAD JUST BEGUN.

PADRAIC CAMPBELL, 1985.   PHOTO TAKEN A MONTH BEFORE
HIS DEATH.

NORA CAMPBELL.   1992.   SHE HAS SPENT A LIFETIME
WITH THE ALEC CAMPBELL STORY.

CHAPTER TWENTY-SEVEN

Preparing for the Executions

When the news went out over the wire services on June 16 that the Board of Pardons had turned down all appeals, a vast throng of reporters from all over country began to descend on Mauch Chunk and on Pottsville. The great theatrical execution of 10 men, stage-managed by the mine owners and the Pinkertons, and acted out by the condemned men, the sheriffs of Carbon and Schuylkill counties with the help of the Coal and Iron Police, the state militia, hundreds of vigilante volunteers, hundreds of reporters, doctors, coroners, juries, as well as thrill-seekers from a dozen states, was scheduled for Thursday morning, June 21, and for the next five days the great bloodbath was the main topic of news all over the country.

Beginning on Monday, June 18, the coverage of the pending executions was huge in all the daily newspapers of the nation and each paper had reporters on location, covering every conceivable angle and filling pages with copy.

The stories written on Monday, June 18 and published the following day rehashed all the cases that the condemned men were involved in: the Jones murder, the Yost murder, the Powell murder, and the Sanger and Uren murders.

James McParland's story at the Alec Campbell trial about the 6,000 AOH lodges located all over the country, each with its secret membership, and all with Molly Maguires in their ranks, was once again held up for public scrutiny. All the secret passwords were described; all the links with the Board of Erin; all the acts of murder and sabotage described.

Interviews with some of the condemned men were in every paper. All except Edward Kelly denied the charges. All said they were innocent; all said that they did not belong to a Molly Maguire organization -- that they belonged to the Ancient Order of Hibernians, which they said was a peaceful fraternal organization. And they said the mine owners and the Pinkertons were out to break the labor union and that they had set up the murders and helped carry them out.

The media would have none of it. They called the men monsters and liars. They called the Irish people prone to crime and violence. They claimed the men had a fair trial and had been proven guilty. They said

151

each man deserved every ounce of agony that was coming his way. All of the newspapers -- the 25 papers that I had read personally -- were unanimous in support of the hanging and all wished that the death the men endured would be slow and hard.

There was a scale of animosity within the overall venom, however, with Edward Kelly, the killer of John P. Jones, having the bizarre status of a "pet," and Alec Campbell as being the one that was despised most. The other eight faced various degrees of hatred, with none coming even close to the pet status of Kelly, and none attracting the unrelenting animosity directed at Alec Campbell.

Kelly was a media darling for two reasons. First, he had been only eighteen when the murder was committed and looked like an innocent 16-year-old. Secondly, he had broken down at the prospect of the gallows and confessed his role in the killing and had asked Mrs. John Jones and God for forgiveness. His youth, his fear and his repentance generated the response in the media that he was the best of a very bad lot, and while nobody wanted him to escape the noose, all wished him an easy death. He did not get it.

Campbell, on the other hand, was self-possessed, strong, iron-willed and he continued to proclaim his innocence. He was bitter only when he talked of Gowen, Packer, Kerrigan and McParland, and he said it was they who set up Jones, not him.

The reporters disliked Campbell's cool courage in the shadow of the gallows, and all -- except one - dismissed his claims of innocence. This reporter, from the *New York Herald*, had a personal interview with Campbell, and while the reporter was obviously hostile to Campbell, he wrote that Campbell was so convincing about his innocence that he "almost believed him."

The Schuylkill County sheriff, J. Werner, conducted himself in a professional manner in the days leading up to the executions and did not let the media hype go to his head. There were 75 journalists in Pottsville and all wanted to go in and interview the prisoners on June 19 and 20 and all wanted to witness the execution in the prison yard, where the gallows had been set up. Sheriff Werner politely but firmly kept the media at bay and would not let any of them in to see the prisoners, and the reporters had to rely on prison staff and relatives of the condemned to describe to them what was going on inside the walls.

Sheriff Raudenbush of Mauch Chunk ran an entirely different operation and allowed the press the run of the prison, and they went from cell door to cell door asking questions of the condemned men and describing everything they saw inside. The gallows at Mauch Chunk were erected inside the prison, in a wide corridor outside the jail cells, and all reporters were told they were welcome to come and see the hanging.

The Pinkertons were everywhere, with Robert Linden and Benjamin Franklin in charge of all of the arrangements for the executions. Franklin and Linden, with the assistance of General Albright, choreographed the hangings in both Mauch Chunk and Pottsville, planning security, bringing in outside sheriffs with expertise at hangings as consultants to the Mauch Chunk and Pottsville sheriffs, and manipulating the media with a steady stream of information, much of it erroneous.

Periodically, during June 18, 19, and 20, the Pinkertons would issue statements about intelligence its undercover agents had found about plans the Mollies had to attack the Pottsville and Mauch Chunk jails in order to free their comrades.

Linden and Franklin said there were thousands of Mollies up in the hills and an attack could occur at any moment. Sheriff Werner and Sheriff Raudenbush said that any reporter let into the jails for the executions would be deputized and armed and might have to fight for his life. All of this was reported in highly colorful prose in the newspapers, and the readers around the country could not be blamed for thinking that a major military confrontation was about to take place in Pennsylvania.

Yet, any person who goes down and takes a look at either the Pottsville or the Mauch Chunk jails today will instantly see how absurd the whole campaign of hysteria really was. The walls of the Pottsville jail are 25 feet high and ten feet thick and the main gate is a massive cast iron barricade. The place could easily withstand a barrage of field artillery or the heaviest cannon balls, and even if 1,000 Mollies attacked it with muskets, a dozen men armed with grenades could easily repel them.

The Mauch Chunk jail is just as formidable. The building is set against a cliff and its massive walls, tiny slit windows, and massive iron door make it a fortress. Five well-armed men could hold off an army, and a reporter from the *New York Tribune*, in a moment of sanity, stated this. He also wrote that the Pottsville jail could withstand an earthquake.

All this, notwithstanding, the Pinkertons and the mine owners appealed to the gullibility and the fears of the Welsh and German residents of the area, with the result that they were out in the streets fully armed, prepared to defend their homes against a Mollie assault.

The Pinkertons had drafted all the Coal and Iron Police in the area and assigned them to help guard the jails and they brought scores of Pinkerton agents in to stage-manage all other activities.

One major irony emerged from the presence of 50 Coal and Iron police at Mauch Chunk jail. These police were employees of the Lehigh Wilkes Barre Coal Company, the same company that had employed John P. Jones, the murdered mine boss, and the same company that provided its legal chief, General Charles Albright, to be chief prosecutor of Alec Campbell and all the others convicted in the Jones killing.

The Lehigh and Wilkes Barre Coal Company could afford to have 50 of its police on hand to ensure that Alec Campbell did not escape the gallows, and yet, this same company, when it was warned that Jones, its employee, was going to be killed at 7:00 a.m. on September 3, 1875, could not find a single policeman to walk him to work and save his life.

It was very obvious that the death of Alec Campbell was infinitely more important to Charles Parrish than the life of John P. Jones.

Beginning on June 19 and continuing into the next day, the relatives of the condemned men in both Mauch Chunk and Pottsville poured into the prisons in large numbers to bid final farewells to their loved ones. Scenes of uncontrollable grief were exhibited in both jails as the relatives realized that time was running out and that the son, brother, father or husband sitting in that cell would soon die at the end of a rope.

Mrs. James Carrol came into the Pottsville jail on June 19 with four small children in tow and she could not control her tears when she saw her husband. Carrol, who was 33, tried to console her but was not able to, and she and the children cried all of the time they were there.

Carrol, like Alec Campbell, had been president of an AOH division -- Carrol's was in Tamaqua -- and like Alec Campbell he had owned a tavern. He had in fact owned the tavern Alec Campbell had owned when he lived in Tamaqua and had bought it from Campbell when Campbell moved to Lansford.

Kerrigan said Campbell and Carrol were related by marriage and both were in fact close friends. Kerrigan had also tied both Carrol and Campbell to the murders of Yost and Jones and had claimed that these two men had been the masterminds behind both murders.

But there was a great deal of uneasiness in even police circles about the guilt of James Carrol and there was a great deal of speculation that the governor might give Carrol, Duffy and Campbell a last-minute reprieve, but this was obviously only speculation.

Thomas Duffy, like James Carrol, was born in the United States of

Irish parents, and the consensus was right up to the final hour that he would be reprieved. A legend exists in the region that the governor had sent a reprieve, but it arrived as Duffy was swinging at the end of a rope.

Duffy had been roughed up several times by police officer Benjamin Yost and he was accused and convicted of getting James Kerrigan, Hugh McGeehan, James Boyle, and James Carrol to set up and carry out the murder of Yost.

Kerrigan had put all the blame on Duffy on the witness stand, and this version was accepted by the jury.

But McParland in his testimony had pointed the finger at Kerrigan, the informer, as the prime mover, and while he implicated Duffy, he did not say he instigated the crime. The defense had a score of witnesses who said they heard Kerrigan threaten to kill Yost, and Kerrigan's own wife had come forward and swore that it was Kerrigan and Kerrigan alone who had killed Yost, and that Duffy, Carrol, Campbell, McGeehan, Boyle and Roarity had nothing to do with the crime.

Duffy's brother Patrick had petitions signed by thousands of people, among them four jurors who had found him guilty but had now changed their minds, and sent these petitions off to the governor, but had received no response.

Duffy had been confident all along of a reprieve, and most of the Pottsville prison officials had also believed he would not hang, but as the hours marched rapidly up to execution time, Duffy had lost his self-confidence and was facing the obvious truth -- that he was going to die.

Duffy was visited by his brother Patrick, his mother and father on June 19 and they did their best to console one another.

James Boyle was also American born and he was very distraught at his predicament. He and his wife wept together in his cell and she told a reporter that if God rewarded people for suffering for the crimes of others then she was confident he would go to Heaven.

Hugh McGeehan, the 25-year-old accused of being the man who shot Yost in exchange for the killing of John P. Jones, was born in Donegal, and like Alec Campbell was very bitter at Kerrigan and McParland. He told his jailers he had nothing to do with the Yost killing, had nothing to do with the Jones killing, and that it was his new in-laws, not Alec Campbell who had given him the money to set up his tavern.

"Keep your heart up, Hugh," said his wife. "You'll die innocent. If you were let out, the Pinkertons would follow you and shoot you down like a dog."

Mrs. James Roarity, who like her husband hailed from Dungloe, County Donegal, spoke only Gaelic, and she talked tearfully to her husband and three children in the jail.

Roarity also spoke English and he seemed bewildered by his predicament. He did his best to comfort his family, but the agony in his eyes was obvious.

County Mayo-born Thomas Munley was visited by his wife and four children and they all prayed together. Munley said he did not want them to come back again the following day -- June 20 -- or on the morning of the execution -- June 21 -- because it was too hard on them and it was too hard on him. He insisted on saying good-bye and they did so and left him and went home in tears.

All during June 19, two priests were giving spiritual comfort to the men. These were Rev. D. J. McDermott, pastor of St. Patricks, Pottsville, and the Rev. M. J. Gately, his assistant.

McDermott had been a bitter foe of the Ancient Order of Hibernians for years, for two reasons. First of all, the AOH was a secret organization, like the Freemasons and a number of other benevolent fraternities, and it had secret rituals like the Masons. The Vatican had prohibited membership in all secret societies, especially the Masons, which was anti-Catholic, and the church had demanded for years that the AOH organization be an open one or its members would face excommunication. The AOH had ignored the church, claiming the church's demands violated its member's civil rights, and had gone on its way.

The second reason that the church was incensed at the AOH was that in the coal regions its members who were miners were the most pro-union, anti-capitalist in the area, and they openly led strikes and were suspected of being the ringleaders among miners who committed acts of sabotage against the mine owners and the railroads. Miners of all nationalities were involved in this activity, but the Irish -- especially the AOH -- got most of the blame, and the church, which had historically, both in Ireland and in the United States, taken the side of the establishment in any major confrontation between the haves and the have-nots, once again sided with the establishment. The priests were prodded on by the English-born Archbishop Woods of Philadelphia, who was a convert from Protestantism and who had publicly condemned the AOH. Woods was also a close friend of Franklin Gowen, who contributed to many of Woods' favorite charities.

However, the manner in which the trials had been conducted, and the open prejudice against the Irish, had given some of these priests second thoughts, and in spite of the excommunication decree in force against the AOH, McDermott and Gately openly consoled the condemned men in Pottsville and allowed them all the sacraments, as if they were Catholics in good standing with the church. The bishops may not have been happy about this but they knew the mood of the Irish in the area, and did nothing about the priests' activities.

Meanwhile out in the yard of the Pottsville jail, the sheriff and his men were busy putting together the gallows, which was constructed of unpainted pine. The platform was 7'9" off the ground and it had three sets of uprights that were 16'4" above the ground. Three cross beams were anchored to each set of uprights and from each cross beam dangled two 1/2" ropes made from Italian hemp. The ropes were donated by a Philadelphia rope maker who had asked that a sign be placed on the gallows, giving the name of the donor, as an advertisement, but the sheriff refused and the donor remained anonymous.

Kate Boyle, a beautiful young Irish girl, who had testified for Thomas Munley, who had been convicted of the murder of Sanger, had been given a long sentence with hard labor for perjury, and she was in the Pottsville jail and could look out and see the gallows being constructed which would kill Munley and her cousin James Boyle.

Kate Boyle was only one of a score of witnesses for the defense who had been jailed after they testified. Three of Alec Campbell's defense witnesses, including William Callaghan, a Donegal-born saloon owner from Mahoney Plane, who had said McParland had boasted about his involvement in a number of murders, had been thrown in jail after he testified. Callaghan also said McParland was a foul-mouthed drunk whom he had thrown out of his saloon several times, and he was so convincing that he annoyed the mine owners and they decided to pay him back. He was in Mauch Chunk jail.

Sheriff Werner said he was going to move all the women away from the window cells during the executions of the six men, but the male prisoners with window cells facing the yard could watch.

Sheriff Werner had not called in the state militia to maintain order. He said he would be able to defend the prison with the help of the Coal and Iron Police, and Robert Linden, in his dual role of captain in the Coal and Iron Police and supervisor with the Pinkertons, said all his men were determined to die at their posts and would never surrender to attacking Mollies. He said he would die by their side.

Over in Mauch Chunk, Sheriff Raudenbush had asked for help from the governor and several companies of the state militia began to enter the town on June 19. Among them were Company F, Fourth Regiment, which arrived in the afternoon under the command of Captain J. Hitzer, who marched up Broadway in full battle gear. Later, Captain M. Jones led 100 members of the Easton Greys into Mauch Chunk and they deployed inside and outside the jail.

Asa Packer had arranged for former Deputy Sheriff Salter of Philadelphia to come up to Mauch Chunk and show Sheriff Raudenbush how to hang the four men because Salter had had a great deal of experience with hangings and Raudenbush had not.

On the afternoon of June 19, Salter met Raudenbush and his aides in the office of the jail and coached them on how to hang a man. Linden, Franklin, Packer and General Albright were also present.

Salter put particular emphasis on the placement of the rope. He used one of the sheriffs deputies as a model in order to show how the noose should be placed and on which area of the neck the knot should be.

Outside the office, in the jail corridor, carpenters arrived early in the morning and began to construct the gallows -- directly outside Alec Campbell's cell. The platform would be fitted across the corridor between the doors to cell 14 on the right and cell 13 on the left. Campbell was in cell 8, three cells down from the platform and he could hear the hammering all day and see the construction out the barred window on the cell door. Campbell would be moved to cell 14 late in the evening of the 20th and Doyle would be placed in cell 12 beside him. Across the hall Donahue would be placed in cell 13 and Kelly in cell 11. All four would be taken from these cells to the gallows.

Campbell was furious at the construction of the gallows in the hallway and even more furious that the construction was beginning on June 19, two days before the execution. He complained bitterly to the reporters about it.

The Carbon County jail had a small yard surrounded by a high wall at that time -- the wall has since been pulled down to make a parking lot -- and the gallows could have been constructed there but the sheriff wanted the hangings done inside, "for security reasons."

Campbell complained that his relatives would see the gallows when they came to visit him on June 19 and 20 and it would badly upset them.

"There is no need for this," he said on the June 19. "They could put that thing up tomorrow night when everybody left. Even if they took all

158

night, who is going to sleep anyway? Who wants to sleep on a night like that?"

But Campbell's complaints were ignored and the sawing and hammering went ahead as scheduled.

Mrs. Alec Campbell saw the gallows when she came to visit her husband the afternoon of June 19 and became hysterical. She screamed and banged her head against the wall and Annie and Sarah Campbell who were with her also began to weep. Campbell was chained to the wall of his cell and could not come and comfort them, but he told them to come inside the cell where they would not see the gallows.

Benjamin Franklin, Robert Linden, Asa Packer and Sheriff Raudenbush, who had been in the office getting educated on some of the more complex points of hanging by Deputy Sheriff Salter, came out when the uproar developed around Mrs. Campbell. They watched without interfering and went back to the office when Mrs. Campbell went into her husband's cell.

Mrs. Mary Campbell, who was described by all of the national reporters as young and very beautiful, came out of the cell later and told reporters that her husband was being murdered, and that she cursed all those who had anything to do with the hanging, especially Gowen, Packer, Pinkerton, McParland and Kerrigan. She said the Irish in the area were no good if they did not do something about the murder that was about to take place and that she hoped a "bucket of blood" would be spilled for every drop of Alec's blood that was spilled.

The reporters headed off immediately for the telegraph office and next day, June 20, the nation's newspapers were full of stories about this "ferocious" Molly wife, who was demanding "buckets of blood." Only one paper, the *Philadelphia Inquirer*, said the hysteria of this young woman, with a year-old child in tow, was understandable given all that she had to endure.

John Donahue, nicknamed Yellow Jack because of reddish-blonde hair, sat in his cell across the hall from Campbell. Stoic and silent, he received his wife and eight weeping children with little display of emotion. He, too, said he was innocent of the murder of Morgan Powell but he would not talk to the press about it and ignored all questions fielded at him from the door of his cell. He spent most of his time praying, but he occasionally talked to Alec Campbell. The media portrayed him as the "tough guy" -- a hard man who would never show weakness.

Doyle was dying of tuberculosis and most believed he would not have

159

lived a month beyond his date with the hangman. Doyle was nervous and emotional, and while he was accused of being the person who shot John P. Jones, in the company of Edward Kelly and James Kerrigan, he denied being involved.

Doyle, who was American-born, was visited by his father, mother, brother and two sisters on June 19. They all tried to comfort one another as much as possible. At one point, they all said the Rosary together.

Kelly said he took part in the killing of Jones but he did not implicate Doyle, just Kerrigan, and he said nothing at all to say about Alec Campbell.

Kelly tearfully asked God for forgiveness before he died and he also asked to see Mrs. John P. Jones, so he could ask her forgiveness.

Mrs. John P. Jones did come to see Edward Kelly on June 19, accompanied by her brother-in-law, Edward Jones, and her two sisters-in-law, Mrs. Faux, who lived across the street from Alec Campbell on Ridge Street in Lansford, and Mrs. James, who lived next door to Alec Campbell.

Kelly tearfully asked for forgiveness, and Mrs. Jones, who was as feisty as Mrs. Campbell, said she hoped God would forgive him. Edward Jones looked at the boy and said, "If it makes you feel any better, I forgive you."

The Jones party then went to inspect the gallows; they walked under the platform and looked at the trapdoor then they mounted the gallows and jumped up and down on the platform.

"It seems good and strong," said Mrs. Jones. "It will probably do the job."

Next they went to the cell of Michael Doyle and looked in the open door.

When Doyle's mother saw her, she shouted, "Get out of here. Go home. You have no right to be here."

Mrs. Jones replied, "I have every right to be here, and if your son had stayed at home, my husband would be alive."

When Doyle's sister advanced on her, Mrs. Jones moved to the open door of Alec Campbell's cell but said nothing and then turned and left the prison.

The sheriff evicted all the newspaper reporters and told all the sightseers who were in the jail to leave by six and all the relatives to leave by seven. After they had left Deputy Sheriff Salter began to test the effectiveness of the gallows by dropping sand bags tied with a noose.

160

Again and again there was the sound of the trapdoors banging against the frame of the gallows, followed by a crunch as the ropes and the crossbeam suddenly took the full weight of the falling bags.

Though they could plainly hear it, neither Campbell, Kelly, Donahue nor Doyle reacted to the fine-tuning of the gallows outside their door, according to the jailors. However, Thomas Fischer, under a death sentence for the murder of Powell but not due to die on June 21, became completely unravelled. Fisher wept and threw up and begged God for mercy. The sheriff and his deputies ignored him and Campbell at one point yelled at Fischer to, "Get a hold of yourself." But Fischer remained a nervous wreck for months, until the hour the hangman put an end to his agony.

That night, their next to last night on earth, the prisoners ate the usual prison supper -- a thick slice of oat bread spread with molasses, accompanied by a cup of tea.

CHAPTER TWENTY-EIGHT

The Eve of The Execution

June 20 dawned cool and windy, with rain clouds in the sky, and mounting tension in both Mauch Chunk and Pottsville. This was the last full day before the executions and the entire population of the area was in a high state of excitement.

Mrs. Alec Campbell began the day by going to the telegraph office and sending a telegram off to Governor Handranft begging him to intervene on behalf of her husband, who, Mrs. Campbell wrote, was innocent. "You can't let it happen," she wrote.

Although the governor did not respond, a staff member in the telegraph office spread the rumor that Mrs. Campbell had been in touch with the governor and the governor was going to pardon Alec Campbell. The rumor spread like wildfire throughout the coal fields, creating even more excitement.

Beginning in the early morning, a steady stream of people called on the Campbells, bringing food, giving the little daughter money, and offering help. There were so many people that they were lined up outside all day waiting their turn to go in.

Mrs. Faux and Mrs. James, the sisters of John P. Jones who were neighbors of the Campbells, watched the growing crowd from behind closed doors with apprehension. But no trouble occurred.

A *New York Times* reporter talked to the Irish who lived in the area to get their opinions of the impending executions.

All were bitter over the executions and said the trials were completely unfair. They said the prejudice against the Irish was unbelievable, and that the juries had all been stacked with Welsh and Germans. They said all the killings were set up by the mine owners and the Pinkertons in order to break the mining laborers union, and that the mine owners wanted to terrorize the union into submission.

The *New York Times* reporter faithfully reported all this and stated that those who spoke to him seemed sincere.

But then he went on to write that the "mere ignorant Irish" did not understand the law and that they were not able to understand the concept of an accessory, thinking that only those who pulled the trigger were guilty, and that they thought men like Campbell, Carroll, Roarty, McGeehan, Boyle, Duffy and Munley were innocent because they were not present when the shots were fired. He said the "mere ignorant Irish" -- which included the Irish-born as well as Irish-Americans -- were not used to living by the rule of law and did not understand complex concepts. The rest of the American population did understand these concepts, of course, he said.

The sister and brother of James Roarty came early in the day to the Pottsville jail, bringing with them a letter they had received from their father in Ireland. Roarty's wife was not with them; she would arrive later in the day.

Sheriff Werner of Pottsville warned all the reporters that they were not to publish the names of any of his staff involved with the executions and he said any reporter who did would be endangering the lives of those who were named.

The sheriff would not give any information about who had made the scaffold and all he would say was that it had been manufactured out of town. But rumor had it the gallows had been made in Pottsville by a carpenter whose name was not published.

The plan originally had been to hang all six prisoners at Pottsville at the one time, but the sheriff was afraid he would bungle the executions trying to hang so many men, and so he decided to hang them two at a time. Besides, he did not want to give the media the idea that he was conducting a massacre of Irish prisoners.

Even though Sheriff Werner seemed to be a little publicity shy, Roland Kline, an undertaker with a coffin showroom on Market Street, was eager for publicity.

Kline had come into the prison on June 19 to measure all six prisoners for their coffins, which he delivered to the prison on the evening of the June 20, and they were stored behind a curtain in the yard.

However, before he brought the coffins up to the jail on the evening of June 20, Kline had displayed the coffins in the window of his showroom all that Wednesday afternoon. Each coffin had a little sign: McGeehan 6': Roarty 5" 10"; Boyle 6"; Duffy 5' 8"; Munley 5' 6"; Carroll 5' 10".

The families of the condemned men had to pass Kline's showroom on the way up to the jail and they no doubt saw the undertaker's idea of a self-promotion only too well.

William Taggart, a prominent coal mine operator in the area, came into town in the late afternoon and said his miners and laborers had all walked off the job and he had heard that they were up in the hills getting ready to invade Pottsville and Mauch Chunk.

Shortly afterwards two companies of militia arrived in town -- the Gowen Guards and the Pottsville Light Infantry. The Gowen Guards were, of course, recruited by Franklin Gowen, and the Pottsville Light Infantry were reporting to Pinkerton boss Robert Linden. Since there was not a single Mollie in sight anywhere, all this extra fire power would seem to have been for the benefit of the media.

The sheriff said all visitors had to be out of the prison by 4 p.m. and that only the clergy would be allowed in after that. He said that any family member who wanted to say good-bye to the prisoners could do so between 6 a.m. and 8 a.m., and that masses would be attended by the prisoners at 7 a.m. and 7:30 a.m. He said all members of the sheriff's jury, the press, and all other guests would not be admitted until 8:30 a.m., and that the executions would take place sometime between 10 a.m. and 3 p.m.

After all the relatives had gone home for the evening, or had found refuge in friendly private residences in the area, the streets of Pottsville became remarkably calm. There were 100 members of a sheriff's posse on the streets fully armed; there were 100 or more Pinkertons; there was a 100-man force organized by the Chief Burgess; there was Gowen's Guards and the Pottsville Light Infantry; and there were scores of Coal and Iron Police.

But there were very few civilians, and of these most were reporters. And there was no sign of the miners who had walked off their jobs, and not a single person that could be identified as a Molly Maguire.

Throughout the night all was quiet in Pottsville.

* * *

The Mauch Chunk gallows were made of well-seasoned oak and were ready on the morning of June 20 and the hemp ropes had been cut to size and were stored in the sheriff's office. White cotton hoods had been made by an unnamed local seamstress and these were stored beside the ropes.

Sheriff Raudenbush could now leave the rest of the final details for his aides to take care of, and he could occupy himself with decisions that needed his immediate attention.

The sheriff was being besieged by requests for admission tickets to the hanging the following day and to date he had received 500 such requests. But the capacity of the Carbon County jail corridor was 150 people at most, and since he was determined to allow the 50 reporters who had arrived in Mauch Chunk to watch the executions, this left only 100 places for everybody else, which included juries, Pinkertons, judges, doctors, prosecutors and other VIPs. He had a problem.

The Campbell family and relatives of the other condemned men arrived in the early afternoon and once again there were shrieks of despair as the women saw the gallows. The reporters, unlike the media at Potts-ville, were once again given the run of the place, and so were members of the Jones family, who were walking up and down the cell block looking in at the prisoners and walking on top of the gallows.

Mrs. Jones had her 17-year old son Edward with her and she asked the sheriff in front of the reporters if she could pull the rope that would release the trapdoor and send the four men into eternity. She said she thought it was her right. The sheriff said that that was his job and that he could not let her do it.

Mrs. Jones then said that perhaps the sheriff did not feel it proper for a woman to do such a thing and if this was so would he let her son Edward act as hangman. Edward said he would consider it a privilege and indeed would even pay a lot of money in order to be the executioner. The sheriff said no.

Mrs. Jones then asked General Albright, who was also present, if he would force the sheriff to comply with her wishes, and he said he would not, because it would not look right.

The sheriff had decreed that all final farewells take place on the after-noon of June 20, because nobody was being allowed into the jail after 6 p.m. and that no relatives would be allowed into the jail the following morning until after the executions had taken place.

While the relatives were there early in the afternoon the Mauch Chunk undertaker came to measure each man for his coffin. Kelly's sister fainted during this proceeding.

Judge Samuel Dreher, the judge who had sentenced all four to death, issued an order to all saloons in Mauch Chunk to sell no liquor until Friday morning. He said he was afraid the Irish would get drunk and cause trouble.

The Pinkertons issued a statement in the afternoon that thousands of people were in the hills above Lansford and Mauch Chunk, and they told Judge Dreher, General Albright and Sheriff Raudenbush to get their families out of town. They complied.

A curfew was announced for 9 p.m., and the residents of the area were told that anyone found out after that time would be assumed to be a Molly Maguire and treated accordingly. Mauch Chunk was an armed camp.

Mrs. Alec Campbell, and Alec's two sisters and his brother James came to say good-bye, and once again Mrs. Campbell was hysterical. According to the media, Campbell was stoic and did his best to comfort his relatives.

While all the relatives were there, including Donahue's wife and eight children, the sheriff opened the front door and let more than a hundred people into the jail corridor, including men, women and teenagers.

Raudenbush had become under increased pressure for tickets to the execution, and since he was not able to comply with all the requests, he decided to let some of these people in to get a preview.

As the relatives watched in bewilderment, the mob came strolling down the cell block, staring into the cells at the prisoners and prancing around on the scaffold.

A Presbyterian minister from Hazelton, who had eight teenage girls with him, gave the girls a guided tour of the scaffold, explaining to them how it worked. While the clergyman was under the platform explaining how the trapdoor worked, another group of youngsters began an impromptu square dance on the platform above, and the trapdoor suddenly fell, bowling the clergyman over and throwing him against the side of the scaffold. He got away with a number of bruises and a half inch cut on his head.

Other local people on the gallows mimed a man being strangled by the noose, while others gave a parody of a condemned man's last words -- delivered with stage-Irish accents.

The sheriff and his men watched all of this without stopping it, and the antics continued until all were evicted at 6 p.m.

Most of the newspapers did not report this incident but four of them did, and those that did questioned the Presbyterian clergyman's taste and the sheriff's judgment. But the incident only merited a few paragraphs at most.

Alec Campbell complained once again to reporters about his trial and said that he had nothing to do with the murder of Jones.

The Irish of Carbon County were in open sympathy with Alec Campbell and told this to every reporter who asked them. The *New York Times* said this sympathy was hard to understand given the nature of Campbell's crimes and that it reflected on the morality of the Irish.

The sheriff displayed a new black suit that he had purchased for Donahue, because Donahue was penniless and his clothes were in tatters. The sheriff said it was not decent to hang a man dressed in this manner.

Raudenbush also said he was personally paying to have the bodies of Kelly and Donahue shipped to their home towns for burial as both families were destitute. He said Kelly's body would be sent to Mt. Laffee with Doyle's and that Donahue's remains would be sent to Tuscarora. Alec Campbell's family said they did not want any assistance from the sheriff.

Mrs. Alec Campbell, Sarah and Annie Campbell, and James Campbell, were the last of the relatives to leave. They all hugged and kissed Alec and then went out into the streets of Mauch Chunk.

As they were leaving, Sheriff Randenbush said to Mrs. Campbell that he was sorry for the trouble the family was in. She ignored him but James Campbell turned to him and said, "Shut up, hangman."

Shortly after 8 p.m, four coffins of white pine were delivered to the jail and placed in the jail parlor.

The prisoners were served a final supper of tea, bread and molasses, and the sheriff told each prisoner to expect a visit from him about 9 a.m. the following morning.

The four Catholic clergymen who had been spiritual advisors to the men, Father Wynn, Father Bunce, Father McElhone and Father Herren, said the Rosary and then left for the night.

The prisoners were allowed to keep a candle burning all night but two guards were posted outside each cell, and two more stood all night on the gallows.

CHAPTER TWENTY-NINE

Day of the Rope

June 21, 1877, a day long remembered by the Irish of Pennsylvania, dawned cool and cloudy, with intermittent showers. The reporters and special guests assembled outside the Pottsville jail in the early morning hours hoped that the rain would hold off until after the day's activities. Except for a few brief showers, the weather did hold up.

The events that were to occur in Pottsville and in Mauch Chunk were carefully scripted by all parties to the drama, including the condemned men, and each player in this theatrical piece was determined to play his part with utmost care, so that the audience who would witness the event first hand, and the nationwide audience who would witness it through the eyes of the media would know that he had given an outstanding performance.

For the Pottsville sheriff and his deputies, the challenge was to put on a dignified, well-choreographed execution, which would portray the sheriff and his aides as strong, capable, humane civil servants, who performed a terrible public service with professionalism and with a certain sense of -- style. Each second of the execution procedure from the jail cell to the final drop had been planned in detail, and on this final hour Sheriff Werner was very nervous that all would go well. He had no fear now of attacking Mollies -- just a terror that he would blunder and look like a fool before the whole world.

To the Catholic clergy, the challenge was to appear solicitous of the condemned men and their families, while avoiding any suggestion whatsoever that they were sympathetic to the AOH or the more violent element in the miners organization. Archbishop Woods of Philadelphia and Bishop O'Hara of Scranton had excommunicated all those who were members of the AOH and the clergy were on a tightrope and knew they risked damnation in the media if they uttered one word of support for the Mollies, but knowing their flock they knew they would lose most of them if they did not comfort the condemned men in their final hours. This was a role that required an adept performance.

168

The condemned men had the most difficult role of all to play; however, each knew that the quality of his performance would be subject to the most minute scrutiny, and criticism of it would be reported nationwide and would reflect on their parents, their sisters and brothers, and on their children and their childrens' children. Their challenge was to face the hangman without fear and die like men, in the classic Irish ethos of facing one's fate without tears and without any plea for mercy directed at an executioner. And each of these ten men, the six at Pottsville and the four at Mauch Chunk were determined to "die game."

Preparations for the Pottsville executions began much earlier than those at Mauch Chunk. At Pottsville, two masses were celebrated in an empty cell at 7:00 a.m. and 7:30 a.m. The Rev. McDermott celebrated the 7:00 a.m. mass for Duffy, Carrol, Roarity and their relatives. The 7:30 a.m. mass was celebrated by Rev. Gately for Boyle, Munley and McGeehan and their families.

The last rites of the church were conducted and all six men were given absolution for their sins so they could die in a state of grace.

James Carrol had prepared a written statement and he asked Rev. McDermott to read it to the reporters before the execution. McDermott said he would.

At 9:05 a.m. McDermott called the press together and read Carrol's statement. The statement, in essence, was a total denial of any involvement in the murder of Jones or Yost. Carrol claimed that Kerrigan was the only one he had ever heard threaten Yost. Carrol claimed he would die an innocent man.

After McDermott had finished reading the statement he paused and stared up at the cloudy skies for a moment, then he spoke again, choosing his words very carefully and delivering them slowly but with emphasis.

"I have been spiritual advisor to Thomas Duffy and James Carrol since they came here. I have heard their confessions and I have been their closest confidant. What I am going to say now is what I feel I must say, and that is this: I know, beyond all reasonable doubt, Duffy was not a party to the murder of Benjamin Yost, and I think the remark will apply with equal force to James Carrol." Having said that, he turned away and walked back into the prison.

McDermott's remarks created a sensation. The priest had a long record of condemning the AOH and all who belonged to it and his remarks carried a great deal of credibility. Since his remarks could not at this late date save the men from the gallows, it was obvious that he spoke as a matter of conscience.

However, the implications of McDermott's statement went well beyond Carrol and Duffy. It also had implications for Alec Campbell's guilt or innocence because the entire prosecution case rested on the allegation that Carrol and Duffy had asked Campbell to arrange to have Roarity, Boyle and McGeehan kill Yost. In exchange Carrol had Kerrigan, Kelly and Doyle kill Jones. According to the prosecution, Carrol and Campbell were not just partners in crime, they were Siamese twins. Now, here was this priest at this late hour saying Carrol was innocent, which implied that Alec Campbell was also innocent.

* * * *

The 200 guests invited to the executions were allowed into the prison yard at 9:30 a.m. and were sheparded to the east corner of the yard where the three sets of gallows had been erected. A large area had been roped off for these guests 30 feet back from the platform and all were told to stay behind the ropes.

Among those present were Benjamin Franklin; George Banks, the Pinkerton superintendent from New York; George R. Kaercher, the Schuylkill district attorney who had prosecuted the six men; Judge Cyrus L. Pershing, who had pronounced the death sentences; and Colonel J. Farr, a special representative of the governor. Farr's presence had generated speculation that he had brought a reprieve for Duffy and Carrol, but he dispelled all hope by saying he was just there to observe.

Patrick Collins, a Pottsville borough commissioner was also present. He received a great deal of attention from the press because Alec Campbell had campaigned for him in Pottsville in September, 1975, and helped him defeat one of Gowen's friends.

At 10:52 a.m. the door from the prison into the yard opened. Sheriff Werner, Deputy Sheriff John Snyder, Keeper of the Prison Moses Innes walked out, followed by Dr. Salladay of Pottsville, Dr. Layer of Tremont. Following them were Hugh McGeehan, with the Rev. Martin Welsh of Heckersville, and James Boyle, with Rev. Beresford of Port Carbon.

McGeehan and Boyle were both dressed in new suits and immaculately groomed. Each held a red rose in his hand. Both walked firmly and held their heads high. McGeehan wore a new pair of boots and the *New York Tribune* reporter noted that the two men looked and acted as if they were going out for the evening.

170

The party mounted the gallows. McGeehan and Boyle were positioned beside marks on the gallows platform, a dangling noose hanging beside each man. They stood silently as the priests read final prayers; McGeehan playing with the noose and Boyle calmly sniffing the red rose. When the priests finished their prayers both Boyle and McGeehan put their roses in their lapels.

Sheriff Werner stepped forward and asked the men if they had anything so say. Each replied that they had nothing to say.

Werner then shook hands with each man as the priests left the platform. Sheriff's aides then quickly strapped the wrists of each man behind his back with leather straps and then pinioned their ankles together.

Werner placed a noose around each man's neck and a white hood over each man's head. Neither man flinched or showed any sign of fear.

Werner and his aides quickly left the platform. There was a moment of complete silence as the Boyle and McGeehan stood there, unflinching, on the edge of eternity. Then suddenly and silently they dropped through the opening as the trapdoor fell away, the impact of the swinging door baffled by cushions mounted on the gallows frame and the two bodies twirled around several feet above the ground.

Boyle seemed to have died immediately, as his body never gave any indication of life after the initial drop. McGeehan seemed to have died easily too, as his body only heaved twice and then was still.

They were cut down at 11:28, and their bodies placed in coffins hidden behind a screen. Then the sheriff and his aides went off to get the next two victims.

At 12:06 p.m., the sheriff and his aides escorted James Carrol and James Roarity out. They were accompanied by the Rev. Gately and the Rev. Beresford. Both were dressed immaculately and each cooly mounted the gallows. They stood there calmly as the priests read prayers and Roarity looked out over the audience, as if searching for someone.

When asked if he had anything to say, Roarity replied, "Well, gentlemen, I want to talk a few words and only a few words. I stand here today before the public and I must say the truth for them. Thomas Duffy is blamed for giving me $10 for shooting a man I never saw -- Benjamin Yost of Tamaqua. Thomas Duffy and I are going to meet with our Lord now and I want to say I never saw Duffy but three times before I saw him in Pottsville jail. What I can say for him is that I never agreed in Tamaqua about Yost or about $10 or anything concerning the thing at all. And another thing I must say for Hugh McGeehan and James Boyle that I

171

never asked them to go over and shoot Yost or any other man, and if they came after me let them say so." [They were already dead but Roarity did not know that.] "I ask forgiveness of the world and of everybody and I hope they forgive me. I hope the Lord will forgive me. I die an innocent man. That is all I have to say."

When it was Carrol's turn he said very quietly but firmly, "I have not much to say except I die an innocent man."

Roarity and Carrol dropped into eternity at 12:16 p.m. They swung several times at the end of the rope but appeared to die quickly and easily. At 12:36 they were cut down and preparations began for the last two.

Duffy and Munley strode out at 1:12 p.m. and each declined to make a statement.

Duffy was calm but he waved away the sheriff when asked for a comment saying, "It is no use saying anything now."

Munley said, "It is too late. . . far too late." But he appeared dignified and unafraid.

They were quickly strapped and hooded and dropped through the trapdoor at 1:24. At 1:37 they were pronounced dead and at 1:48 they were cut down.

The crowd of spectators had watched the execution in silence and they began to disperse immediately at 1:48, talking quietly to one another.

There was a tremendous sense of anti-climax after the massive psychological build-up all week. They had come prepared to experience the horrors of a state-ratified public killing and those who hated the Irish felt cheated because of the cool and courageous way the men had met their deaths. It was like watching a theatrical event that was only make believe and the anti-Irish mob believed they did not get their pound of flesh.

Next day many of the newspapers criticized the dead men for treating their own executions in such a cavalier manner. It was the *New York Tribune's* opinion that it "cheapened" the event.

* * * *

In Mauch Chunk, Sheriff Raudenbush cared nothing for the image he presented to the media and did not focus on such details as putting cushions up that would baffle the sound of the falling trapdoor or providing leather straps to bind the men while they were being executed.

Raudenbush had chained the condemned men to the walls of their cells and he would take them out of their cells and hang them in their

172

chains.

Raudenbush had not protected the men from reporters or other curiosity seekers either -- unlike Werner of Pottsville who did his best to minimize the stress on the condemned men and their relatives.

Raudenbush had made only one concession to any of the prisoners and that was to allow Alec Campbell to have two visitors on the morning of his execution.

Campbell had asked that Barney Gallagher, his brother-in-law who was married to Annie Campbell, be allowed to visit him and that James Sweeney, an uncle of his brother Niall's wife, also be allowed in. They were let in at 7:00 a.m. and were allowed to stay until 8:00 a.m., then they left carrying a last letter for Campbell's wife.

The sheriff had not allowed the priests who had been comforting the condemned men to stay overnight or to arrive early to say Mass. Instead, they were allowed in at 9:30, one hour before the time of execution.

At 10:00 A.M., Raudenbush let in the sheriff's jury, 50 members of the press, a dozen local VIPs, Sheriff Brennaman of Lancaster County, who had volunteered to help hang the men, Coroner Moser of Lehigh County, who had a professional curiosity, a prominent citizen of Philadelphia named Isiah H. Brown, who just wanted the experience, Prosecutors General Albright, F. W. Hughes, and Siewers, Asa Packer, Charles Parrish, Judge S. Dreher, who had pronounced the death sentences, Captain Linden of the Pinkertons, Edward Jones, the brother of John P. Jones, and Daniel Kalbfus, Campbell's lawyer. It was rumored that James McParland was also there, but no reporter was able to state definitely that this was so. In all, the spectators numbered 150.

The door of cell 14 opened at 10:26 and Alec Campbell walked out followed by Rev. James Wynne of Summit Hill, Campbell's confessor. Campbell walked quickly up the steps and across to the left rear of the platform and stood beside the noose.

Doyle walked out of cell 12 -- the cell next to Campbell's -- accompanied by Rev. M. R. Bunce of Mauch Chunk, and walked slowly to the spot at the right rear of the scaffold, facing Campbell. Doyle looked extremely ill from his terminal tuberculosis, and he walked with difficulty.

Next, Donahue came out of cell 13 and walked briskly up to the spot at the left front of the platform, standing side by side with Campbell. Donahue was accompanied by Rev. W. Heiner.

Kelly came out of cell 11, looking nervous, and stood beside Doyle, facing Donahue. He was accompanied by Rev. E. V. McElhone of Lowrytown.

Sheriff Raudenbush asked Campbell if he had anything to say. Campbell looked Raudenbush directly in the eye and said, "I have not an enemy in the world at this moment because I forgive them all. I hope God will forgive me. That is all."

Donahue told the sheriff he had nothing to say. Doyle said something but it was inaudible to the reporters. Kelly started to speak but then seemed to forget what he had wanted to say but the Rev. McElhone prompted him from a note he had in his hand and Kelly repeated after McElhone the words the priest had obviously written for him.

"If I had listened to my priests and bishops and avoided secret societies I would not be here now. I ask God for forgiveness."

The priests then asked the four men to kneel and all were given absolution. After that the priests left the platform and Sheriff Raudenbush and Deputy Sheriff Pealer adjusted the chains around their elbows and ankles and slipped the ropes and the hoods over their necks.

At 10:45 a.m., the doors dropped with a fearsome crash that startled most of the onlookers, and this was followed by a loud crunch as the four falling bodies were pulled abruptly to a halt by the ropes.

Next came a horrendous clanking of chains as the four men twirled around on the end of each rope, each twirling at a different momentum.

Alec Campbell seemed to be knocked unconscious from the first second, because he never moved a finger after the drop. Kelly and Doyle did not appear to put up any fight either. But to the horror of the spectators, Donahue's legs kicked wildly and his hands seemed to be attempting to get up to where the rope was strangling him, and the desperate struggle, accompanied by the clanking of chains, went on for five minutes.

Alec Campbell was not dead, however. After 5 minutes and 30 seconds, Drs. Jones, Irwin, Stoop and Addis checked the pulse of the men. Donahue's was 80; Kelly's was 160; Doyle's was 104; and Campbell's was 109.

Donahue, in spite of his struggle was the first to die at 7 minutes after the drop; Kelly was dead in 10 minutes; Doyle died in 12 minutes, and Alec Campbell's heart continued to beat until 17 minutes after the trapdoor fell. Then it was still.

Dr. Shirmer told the media that all the men had died of strangulation.

* * * *

174

After the men were pronounced dead, the sheriff invited the spectators to come up to the scaffold and examine the hanging bodies. Most of them did.

Edward Jones, the brother of John P. Jones, went up to the body of Campbell and walked around it with, as a *New York Herald* reported noted, a look of ferocious satisfaction.

After 15 minutes of this, the sheriff cut down the bodies and pulled off the hoods. The spectators crowded around to see what effect the hanging had on the features of the dead men.

Doyle had all the skin on his neck ripped off and the hair on one side of his head was gone. Kelly's features were terribly distorted and his eyes bulged and his tongue protruded.

Donahue did not seem to have any marks on him, but there was blood all over the front of his shirt.

Alec Campbell did not seem to be marked at all, and his eyes were closed and his face expressionless.

The spectators who had witnessed the Mauch Chunk executions did not leave with the same feeling of anti-climax that those who had witnessed the execution of the six in Pottsville had experienced.

Although these four men had also died gamely and had conducted themselves with courage, Raudenbush saw to it that their killing was a noisy and seemingly brutal affair, complete with crashing trapdoors and clanking chains. And, of course, there was Donahue's terrible death struggle.

The spectators had also been allowed to see twisted faces and broken skin, so there was a feeling that great pain had been inflicted and revenge imposed. It gave them satisfaction and that satisfaction was reflected in the look of delighted malice on the face of Edward Jones.

Of course, in reality the men at Mauch Chunk may have suffered no more than those at Pottsville, and it was just a case of the stage manager of the event, Raudenbush, deciding that he wanted no antiseptic mercy killing in his jail, so he staged the executions in a way that presented the appearance of a medieval public spectacle.

Raudenbush did not want the bodies lying around his jail however, once he had eliminated the life from them.

Raudenbush and his aides picked up the bodies and put them into the pine coffins, and then sent word across the street to the houses where the relatives of Campbell, Doyle, Kelly and Donahue had been waiting that the bodies would be shipped out shortly from the Mauch Chunk station to the home towns of the dead Mollies. He said a special train was being provided, courtesy of Asa Packer, and that the relatives should come and accompany the bodies.

Alec Campbell's wife, brother and two sisters came to the lobby of the jail to accept his remains. There were no tears in their eyes now, just a bitter resignation.

Sheriff Raudenbush pointed to one of the coffins and said Campbell's body was there, and Mrs. Campbell went over and opened the lid and looked inside. She said nothing, however.

James Campbell stared at the sheriff and told him that they did not want a ride on Packer's train, that they had brought a hearse and would take the body home themselves. Mrs. Campbell, her brown eyes smoldering, told the sheriff they did not want his coffin either. Then she, and the other members of the Campbell family, took Campbell's body out of the coffin and carried it outside to the hearse and wrapped it in a blanket they had brought. They then headed off down the street, walking after the hearse, which was drawn by two horses.

They did not look back at the county jail, or at the sheriff who stood outside it. And they ignored the reporters and all of their questions.

By the time they had reached the court house square, a quarter of a mile down Broadway, a score of Irish people had fallen in behind the Campbells and walked with them. By the time the procession was out of Mauch Chunk, several hundred Irish were part of the procession, and as the hearse passed through Nesquohoning, three miles from Lansford, the parade had two thousand participants. At Ridge St., Lansford, the entire street was choked with people for blocks on each side of the Campbell home, and the biggest wake that Northeastern Pennsylvania had ever seen was about to begin.

Next day the *Philadelphia Inquirer* would call the multitudes who showed up for Alec Campbell's wake "misguided," and the *New York Tribune* would denounce the Irish for honoring the memory of a killer like Campbell. The *Tribune* said the Irish had disgraced themselves.

But the wake went on night and day for three days, with thousands coming from all over the area to attend the wake in his home. On the day of the funeral, on Sunday, June 24, the roads around Lansford were choked with carriages and the *New York Herald* estimated that a total of 10,000 people, marching ten abreast, had followed the hearse from Campbell's house in Lansford to St. Joseph's Church in Summit Hill, one and a half miles away. The *Herald* stated that when the front of the procession was arriving at the church, the rear of the procession was still passing by the Campbell house.

Carbon and Schuylkill counties had never seen or heard of a funeral like that, and for years afterwards the Campbell wake would always be referred to in the media as an example of the lack of respect the Irish had for the law -- because it was believed that only a totally lawless people would have become involved in such a spectacle that honored the memory of an executed murderer.

* * * *

In the aftermath of the executions there were no revenge killings by the Mollies, no public disturbances of any kind, and no word at all of the thousands of Molly Maguires that were supposed to have been in the hills above Mauch Chunk, ready to take a terrible revenge on those who hanged Alec Campbell.

Indeed, there was total silence, which some interpreted to mean that the Molly Maguires had been cowed, but which others interpreted as meaning that there never had been thousands of Molly Maguires -- that they were a phantom organization created by Gowen, Packer and Parrish for their own ends.

For the Campbells the prelude to the executions had been a time of horror; the aftermath had been a time of terrible grief.

James Campbell, who was only 20 when his brother was executed, went first to California and then to Australia. But he was back in Ireland at the turn of the century and he was still there when I was a child -- a colorful old man who talked about everything except the Molly Maguires.

Both Sarah and Annie raised large families but they never really put Alec's execution behind them, and Mrs. Alec Campbell lived until 1905 but died at a relatively early age. Her daughter, Rose, was a teenager before she knew how her father had died.

CHAPTER THIRTY

Additional Executions

The hangings did not end with the executions in Mauch Chunk and Pottsville on June 21, 1877. Ten more men were to be hanged in that area during the next two years, all of them alleged to have been Molly Maguires.

But the media hype and the mass hysteria that had accompanied the 10 executions on June 21st was never repeated. Indeed, from then on there was a growing backlash, even in the rabid anti-Irish newspapers, against a continuation of the executions because in the eyes of many there was a growing awareness that the executions had become legal lynchings.

Perhaps the most controversial of these later executions was the hanging of Jack Kehoe, county delegate of the AOH, on December 18, 1878. Kehoe, who had been hyped up in the media as "King of the Molly Maguires" was a popular tavern owner in Girardville and had also been elected chief of police of that town. Kehoe, like Campbell, had been a power-broker in the politics of the area and had made a mortal enemy of Franklin Gowen. Kehoe and Campbell had persuaded the Irish voters, usually Democratic, to vote for Republican candidate Handranft in the election for governor of Pennsylvania. As a result Handranft beat Judge Cyrus L. Pershing, Gowen's hand-picked candidate. Gowen and Pershing were to even the score with Kehoe in 1876 when Judge Pershing, presiding at Kehoe's trial for murder, sentenced him to death.

Gowen hated Handranft personally and he waged a long vicious campaign against him that continued for years after the election. When Handranft waffled and delayed signing Kehoe's death warrant, Gowen told the media, "Handranft had better hang Kehoe, or I will hang Handranft."

Kehoe had been accused of taking part in the murder of Frank W. Landon, an unpopular mine official who was killed in a brawl at a picnic in 1862, sixteen years before Kehoe was executed.

At the time Landon was killed the incident was viewed as a drunken brawl involving the Irish and the Welsh. Two men were arrested and accused of manslaughter but were acquitted. There was no Molly Maguire connection mentioned until many years later when Gowen and the anti-

Irish media began to use the term Molly Maguire in connection with every crime that was committed in the area.

However, in 1876 when Gowen was desperate to hang Kehoe on some pretext -- any pretext -- he dug up the Landon case, because Kehoe, like scores of other Irish miners, had had a quarrel with him. Gowen managed to get a first degree murder verdict against Kehoe, using a stacked jury and orchestrating the prosecution himself, and in spite of the fact that two other defendants, who admitted taking part in the brawl and were convicted of manslaughter, swore that Kehoe was not involved in the fight at all, Kehoe went to the gallows.

The Kehoe case had nothing to do with the unrest in the mining areas in the 1870s and neither had the other cases involving the execution of several other Irishmen -- even though Gowen presented them all as Molly Maguire crimes.

James McDonnell and Charles Sharp were hanged by Sheriff Raudenbush in Manch Chunk on January 14, 1879, for the murder of mine operator George K. Smith. Clearly this murder was part of a nationwide resistance to the forced conscription into the U.S. Army in 1863, which generated huge riots in New York City that year and other riots all over the country, including one at Cass Township in Schuylkill County.

Basically, those who were rioting were incensed at the idea that they could be drafted into the army when the more affluent could buy their way out simply by paying $300 to the U.S. Government.

The sum of $300 was a small sum to mine owners or to professionals like doctors and lawyers, who made $9,000 - $12,000 per year, a large sum at that time. But $300 was a year's salary to mine laborers, who were mostly Irish, and there was no way a mine laborer could come up with this kind of money. The result was that the laborers believed that they were being used as cannon fodder while the more affluent escaped the draft.

In the mining areas, the mine owners also either won exemptions for favored Welsh mining officials or for favored Welsh miners, while at the same time they had conscripted Irish union activists and had them shipped off to the front.

The result of this was widespread violence and George K. Smith, who was a close friend of General Charles Albright, later to become the prosecutor of the Mollies, was gunned down by a dozen men with blackened faces because he had been an outspoken champion of forced conscription and he had been feeding Albright and other army officials with lists of Irish miners who worked for him who he believed should be drafted into the army.

Albright waited sixteen years before hanging someone for this crime and the pair he selected both denied any involvement.

The execution of these two by Sheriff Raudenbush was an ugly, brutal affair that almost got the sheriff lynched by angry citizens of Mauch Chunk.

There was a widespread resistance in Mauch Chunk to the execution of this pair because it was believed there was no real evidence against them and that they were being hustled off to the gallows as part of the Molly Maguire hysteria.

The lawyer for the pair, an attorney named Longstreet, had gone to the governor the day before the execution and begged him for a stay of execution based on new evidence. The governor said he would think it over and get back to Longstreet the following morning.

Raudenbush had a signed death warrant which instructed him to execute the men between the hours of 10:00 a.m. and 3:00 p.m. on January 14, 1879, and when no word had arrived by 10:00 a.m., Raudenbush began to prepare for the executions, in spite of pleas from the lawyer that he could wait until 2:00 p.m. or even 3:00 p.m.

Raudenbush would not wait and took the men out of their cells and had them up on the gallows platform at 10:20 a.m. when a tremendous banging was heard at the front door of the prison. It was the telegraph operator from the Mauch Chunk telegraph station with a telegram from the governor giving a five-day stay of execution.

Raudenbush told his aides to ignore the uproar at the door and went ahead with the hanging, dropping the two men to their deaths. Only when they had been swinging for five minutes did he open the front door to admit the distraught telegraph operator and a hysterical Mrs. Sharp and Michael McDonnell, the brother of James McDonnell, who saw their kin dangling from the ropes.

McDonnell was still alive when he was cut down, but he died shortly after, and Michael McDonnell tried to assault Raudenbush yelling, "You have murdered my brother."

Mrs. Sharp went berserk and did her best to attack Raudenbush, but he was protected by his aides.

Later, a huge mob gathered outside the prison, all of them calling for Raudenbush's death. It was only when the local parish priest, Rev. Bunce, intervened that the mob became a little less violent. Bunce told the mob he had been at the executions and that the sheriff thought it was Michael

McDonnell and Mrs. Sharp at the door and did not know it was the tele-graph operator.

Nevertheless, two facts remain undisputed: a message from the governor had been expected, and Raudenbush could have legally waited several more hours and did not have to rush the men to the gallows in the way he did.

That was the last "Mollie" hanging in Mauch Chunk and it matched the Alec Campbell execution for brutality.

* * * *

The Molly Maguire tag was also hung on the killing of Alexand Rea in 1868, even though Rea was killed in an armed robbery and the only AOH connection was that one of the accused, Patrick Hester, was an AOH division president when he was arrested in 1876. According to the prose-cution, Hester, Peter McHugh and Patrick Tully had shot Rea during a robbery -- a type of crime very common then as now -- but Hester's later affiliation with the AOH enabled Gowen to claim that this, too, was part of the Molly Maguire conspiracy.

These executions took place in Bloomsburg and were a bloody, grue-some affair. All present acknowledged that Sheriff John W. Hoffman was drunk that day. So drunk he could barely walk.

Hoffman had his aides carry three pine coffins out before the execu-tions took place and had them placed beside the gallows, where the con-demned men could see them on the way out to their deaths.

The execution took place in public and a big crowd showed up, many in a festive mood.

But Sunny Williams, a thirteen-year old girl who with a dozen com-panions had climbed up on a shed to get a view of the proceedings, was killed when the roof of the shed collapsed. Joseph Engst, a Mahoning Valley farmer who was drunk, fell to his death from the roof of the Exchange Hotel, as he watched the executions.

Sheriff Hoffman bungled the executions and the men died very hard. Later, the wedding ring of Pat Hester was stolen from his finger.

Although the Tully, Hester and McHugh executions did not involve union motives, the executions of Thomas Fisher, Martin Bergin, Denis Donnelly and Peter McManus all involved mining supervisors.

Denis Donnelly, the AOH division president of Raven, was accused of having set up the murder of Sanger and Uren, the two mining officials

181

killed on September 1, 1875.

Again, it was James McParland who was the only major witness against Donnelly, and again McParland was accused by the defense of not only planning the murders, but actually taking part in them as one of the gunmen. Donnelly produced a score of witnesses who claimed he was in their presence when the murders were carried out. But Donnelly was hanged and two other men who were very close to McParland and who had taken part in the killings, Thomas Hurley and Frank McAndrews, were allowed to leave the county and escape prosecution.

It is probable that Gowen and the Pinkertons did not want McAndrews and Hurley prosecuted because they would have turned around and pointed at McParland as being the one who set up and carried out the killings as part of the Gowen-Packer- Parrish-Pinkerton plan to get the whole area in an uproar against the AOH and the unions.

The execution of Thomas Fischer, the German-Irish AOH county delegate from Carbon County, for the murder of Morgan Powell had also created a great deal of bitterness in Carbon County.

The evidence against Fischer was almost non-existent and there was considerable lobbying to save him from the executioner but to no avail. He was hanged on March 28, 1878.

The final two executions attributed to the Molly era seem to have been the result of personal grudges rather than any organized attack.

One was the murder of mining clerk Patrick Burns, an Irish-Catholic whom Martin Bergin killed because Bergin claimed he was shortchanging him on the company books. Bergin was hanged in Pottsville on January 16, 1879.

The other was the killing of night watchman Frederick Hesser in what appeared to be a retaliation for real or imagined insults. The killer was Peter McManus, who was executed on October 9, 1879, and he was the last of the so-called Mollies to die on the gallows.

By this time, however, there was no media attention at all for this Molly Maguire execution. The press had already turned their attention to other issues and the whole Molly Maguire hysteria, which began with a great deal of media hype in 1875, drifted into near oblivion by 1879.

But a great deal of passion about the issue still existed and this passion has erupted over the years into great public debates in Pennsylvania over who was the victim and who was aggressor in the great Molly Maguire controversy. The debate still goes on.

CHAPTER THIRTY-ONE

The Aftermath

After the executions and the funerals, the names of the dead Mollies disappeared from the front pages of the nation's newspapers and, except for Alec Campbell, their names were only in the news again when a new book was published on the Molly Maguires and there was a fresh eruption of publicity. But these books were few and years passed without a new one arriving on the scene.

Alec Campbell, because of the legend associated with his hand print on the wall of his jail cell, was in the news in Carbon County right up to 1931 -- 54 years after his execution.

The reason for this was that Campbell's cell at Mauch Chunk had become a tourist attraction, with busloads of people coming from all over to see the cell in person, and this may have continued to the present were it not for the fact that the sheriff in office in 1931 grew tired of the tourists and made the cell off limits to them. Since then, the name Alec Campbell has slipped into the background in Carbon County, although the legend is still mentioned in handouts by the tourist office in the town of Jim Thorpe (Mauch Chunk) and the hand print is still on the wall of the cell.

However, even though the Mollies and their relatives drifted off into anonymity, many of the major players in the Molly Maguire drama would make the news for many years to come, some of them making the front pages.

Gowen had been immensely pleased with the way his campaign against the AOH and the WBA had gone and had openly boasted about it to his English board of directors when he went to report to them in London in May 1877, a month before Alec Campbell's execution.

In a speech before the board he said that he had to break the union in order to save the company and that now "for the first time since we acquired the title, we found ourselves in the real ownership of the lands."

It was very clear during this speech that Gowen was claiming that the AOH, the WBA, and the Mollie Maguires were all one and the same.

But Gowen was boasting too soon, because he immediately got into labor trouble with the Brotherhood of Locomotive Engineers in 1877. In a confrontation with this union, whose membership roster listed few Irish, riots broke out in Philadelphia which took the lives of 30 people.

New strikes soon erupted in the coal mines with Germans, Welsh and Swedes confronting Gowen, Packer and Parrish. In this new violence both miners and mine bosses were shot dead and none of it could be laid at the doorstep of the AOH leaders since they were either dead or in jail.

Gowen tried to ride out the storm, but his company slid into bankruptcy and he was dumped by the English board of directors in 1880. Thus Gowen's dreams of monopolizing the coal mining industry came to an end.

Gowen went into private law practice in Baltimore. It would seem he made a reasonably good living, though it was far removed from the visions of great wealth he had when he was riding high with the Reading Railroad.

Then, in December 1889, in a Washington, D.C. hotel room apparently in good health and good spirits, he placed a gun to his head and pulled the trigger, blowing away half of his face and head. He died instantly.

Many people at first thought that the relatives of the Molly Maguires had evened the score, but an investigation by Robert Linden, then head of the Pinkerton office in Philadelphia, said it was a suicide and the Washington police agreed.

Some said he was destroyed by remorse over the execution of 20 men, but many reject that, saying that he cared nothing for the dead men or their relatives.

Others say he was depressed over the destruction of all his plans and could not face life as an ordinary lawyer.

The reason will probably never be known, but when the word got out in Carbon and Schuylkill counties, the relatives of Alec Campbell and the other executed men wished him an unpleasant eternity in hell.

Most of the other prosecution personalities in the Molly Maguire trials did not have a very agreeable future.

Charles Parrish went bankrupt in 1878.

Asa Packer died suddenly in 1879 and his wife died the following year. His two sons died the year after that, putting an end to the Packer name. The Packer company then went bankrupt.

Sheriff Bessemer, who arrested Alec Campbell in February 1876 and told him he was on his way to the gallows, was dead before Campbell, having died suddenly after the Campbell guilty verdict.

General Albright, who prosecuted Campbell and told the Board of

Pardons in 1877 that it was imperative that Campbell die, was dead himself in 1880, having choked on food and gone into a coma from which he did not recover.

F. Hughes, Gowen's lawyer and Albright's assistant prosecutor, was dead in 1882 from alcoholism and assorted other diseases and wound up talking to himself a great deal.

Allen Pinkerton had a stroke shortly after Campbell's execution and began to go into a physical and psychological decline. By 1880, three years after the execution, he was coherent only part of the time. By 1884 he was senile and a massive stroke killed him.

William. Kaercher, the district attorney in Schuylkill county who had been an employee of Gowen's before the trials and who became Gowen's chief counsel for the Reading Railroad after Hughes died, was severely mangled in a Reading train crash in 1889. It took hours to extricate him from the wreckage and he died hours later in the Pottsville hospital.

Benjamin Franklin, the loyal Pinkerton Philadelphia office chief, expected a big raise in salary after he had arranged the execution of Campbell and the other men, but was instead pushed aside by Pinkerton and his job given to Linden.

And James McParland, the Armagh man whose testimony sent so many of his fellow countrymen to the gallows, what happened to him?

The story is a lengthy one, but it is worth telling. He, too, did not have a happy aftermath to the Molly Maguire episode. Here is what happened.

McParland was named manager of the Pinkerton Denver office after he left Pennsylvania and he continued with the union-busting career he had began back in Pennsylvania. The Pinkertons had lucrative contracts in the West to spy on the Western Federation of Miners and McParland was passionately disliked by all of the miners in that area, who were aware that he had put spies in their midst.

But tragedy had stalked McParland since he left Pennsylvania. First he lost the wife he had met down in Pennsylvania -- Mary Fitzgerald from Schuylkill County -- and then he lost his 12-year-old daughter, who died from an unnamed disease. Frank's son Eneas then came from New Zealand to live with him but he began to drink heavily and was killed in a traffic accident, along with his wife.

McParland then married Mary Regan from Wisconsin. Catherine McParland, Charles McParland's daughter, came to live with them in Denver but McParland was not a happy man.

185

He had reasons for his unhappiness, according to Catherine McParland Schick, who told me about these reasons 60 years later.

One was the fact that he had been badly mauled in court by Clarence Darrow in 1907, when Darrow had confronted McParland on the witness stand during the trial of three Western Federation of Miners officials who had been accused of conspiracy to murder former Governor Frank Stuenenberg of Idaho.

The case had many similarities to the Molly Maguire case, with union officials being accused of murder and the actual murderer -- Harry Orchard -- turning state's evidence and pointing the finger at WFM President Charles Moyer, Secretary Treasurer William Haywood, and WFM member George Pettibone. They were supposed to have been the masterminds behind the murder.

During the trial it got out that Orchard, who had a long criminal record -- like James Kerrigan -- and had been approached by McParland to turn state's evidence and implicate Haywood, Pettibone and Moyer with the promise that he would get off scot free. McParland also quoted the Bible to Orchard and according to Orchard convinced him to give up his evil ways and embrace Christianity. McParland said God would reward him if he implicated Moyer, Pettibone and Haywood.

Orchard began to see things McParland's way and complied with the detective's request to testify against the trio. When Darrow got McParland on the stand he tore his character to pieces, dragging in the Molly Maguire episode in as well.

McParland was humiliated by the treatment he got from Darrow, the most famous trial lawyer in the United States and even more humiliated by the fact that the three defendants were acquitted.

McParland retired shortly after that, but he and the Pinkertons continued to get a great deal of bad publicity for years after because of the Stuenenberg case.

The tragedy for Alec Campbell was, of course, that he did not have a lawyer like Darrow defending him. If he had, he would never have been convicted.

McParland continued to live in Denver at 1256 Columbine Street after he retired, with niece Catherine McParland and wife Mary Reagan McParland.

But he was to lose a leg and then an eye, which Catherine Schick attributed to old injuries from his Molly Maguire days, but which was more likely caused by diabetes or over-indulgence in alcohol -- a lifelong problem.

In the last ten years of his life he descended into a private hell as he became increasingly more paranoid about being assassinated by the descendants of the Molly Maguires.

Catherine McParland Schick said that in the last years of his life he had high walls built around his Denver home and that inside the walls he had attack dogs always on the loose.

In addition, he had bars put on all the lower windows and had a hand gun on every table in the house. He also carried a gun constantly and got up frequently during the night to patrol the house. He died in a hospital bed at Mercy Hospital in Denver in 1918, sick, paranoid, and alone.

Thus ended the life of James McParland long after he had sent Alec Campbell to his grave. He had money and fame, but his life could hardly have been satisfying especially given the horrors he experienced in the end.

Compared to that, Alec Campbell's death was a brief, merciful affair.

* * * *

There was one major player in the Alec Campbell story that had yet to be accounted for and that was attorney Daniel Kalbfus. I decided to find out what had become of him.

I found the answer after an investigation: Kalbfus suffered a psychological breakdown after the execution of Alec Campbell and was incarcerated in an institution for the insane. He died there six months later.

CHAPTER THIRTY-TWO

The Last Word

The final conclusion I had come to about Alec Campbell's guilt or innocence -- namely that he was not guilty from a legal point of view was not a very satisfactory ending to the long investigation I had conducted on the case. But I knew that this was the best I could do. Short of finding a signed confession written by some of the participants in the conspiracy how else could I exonerate Alec Campbell completely?

However, there was more than my inability to prove Alec Campbell's innocence which bothered me about the way the investigation had turned out and that was the number of questions which I had not found any answers for. And it was not just the questions involving James McParland, but all the questions that had emerged as I had gone over the trial transcripts and other material.

I made a list of them, not necessarily in order of importance.

- Why had Alec Campbell's lawyers ignored all the opportunities presented by the prosecution case?
- Why had Kelly and Doyle agreed to shoot Jones? Was it for a financial reward, or was it for some other reason?
- Why did Guss, the two Beards, and Michael Shepp become involved in the conspiracy? Were they rewarded by Packer, Parrish and Gowen?
- Who was responsible for the perjury of some of the defense witnesses? Was it Campbell or was it his lawyers?
- Why was it that the fact that both Charles McParland and James McParland married women they met in Pennsylvania never made public? Did anyone outside the families involved know?
- Was James McParland a major figure in the conspiracy or was he only a minor figure who was made a major figure by the media?
- Was Franklin Gowen the prime mover in the conspiracy against the AOH and the WBA, or was he merely a front man for the powerful Asa Packer? Was he, like McParland, a creation of the media?
- Why had Gowen killed himself?
- Why did almost everyone who was involved in the conviction of Alec Campbell come to a violent end?

188

- What about the handprint on the wall? I got permission to go into the Carbon country jail to look at it. It is still there.
- What about my father's story about Alec innocently lending his gun to Kerrigan? Had this happened, or was this story based on prosecution testimony, and passed on to my father in Ireland? Or had Alec really given the gun in order to get Jones killed?

As I thought about all of these questions, as well as the questions that were raised when I was chasing down McParland's relatives, I wondered if I should continue the investigation -- turning away from the McParland-Pinkerton-Gowen combination which had been the focus of my attention for 15 years -- and perhaps do an in-depth investigation of Asa Packer, Charles Parrish, General Albright, Wallace Guss, James Kerrigan, Daniel Shepp, Michael and Samuel Beard, and discover their exact role in the Alec Campbell case, and why they did what they did.

I did a little further investigation and discovered correspondence between Rev. McDermott of Pottsville and Archbishop Wood of Philadelphia which suggested Wood was giving McDermott a great deal of money and that McDermott was cosy with the Pinkertons -- especially Linden.

I tracked down a great nephew of Franklin Gowen who gave me intriguing information -- that Gowen had gone to Alec Campbell's death cell and offered him his life if he would be a witness against Kehoe. Campbell refused.

But after some more thought I decided I really did not have the staying power to probe any more into this family tragedy, because I sensed that, even if I were to devote the next 15 years to the project, I would have even more unanswered questions than I have now. So, I decided to close the book on the Alec Campbell case, even though I was more than a little disappointed I had not come up with the definitive Molly Maguire story, but had instead come up with another Molly Maguire story and not the last word on the subject.

Still, I had unearthed more information than any other writer and if the truth is the sum total of all of the facts, then I had made a major contribution to the number of facts known about the Molly Maguire episodes, and as a result helped move a little closer to the truth.

It was a very small consolation, but a consolation nevertheless.

Jersey City
June 21, 1993

BIBLIOGRAPHY

I consider the books listed below to be the most important of the many books written on this subject. However, since most of these books, in my opinion, are based on incomplete information, their value may be limited.

Tom Barrett *The Mollies Were Men* (New York: Vantage, 1969)

Anthony Bimba *The Molly Maguires* (New York: International Publishing Co., 1950)

Wayne G. Broehl, TR *The Molly Maguires* (Massachusetts: Harvard University Press, 1964).

J. Walter Coleman *The Molly Maguire Riots* (Richmond: Garrett & Massie, 1936).

F. P. Dewees *The Molly Maguires* (New York: Burt Franklin, 1877).

Arthur Conan Doyle *The Valley of Fear* (New York: George H. Doran Co., 1914)

George Korson *Minstrels of the Mine Patch* (Philadelphia: 1938)

Arthur H. Lewis *Lament for the Molly Maguires* (New York: Harcourt Brace & World, 1964).

Edward Winslow Martin *The History of the Great Riots and of the Molly Maguires,* (Philadelphia: National Publishing Company, 1877). Reprinted 1971 by Augustus M. Kelly Publishers, New York

Allan Pinkerton *The Molly Maguires and the Detective* (New York: Dover, 1877)

The following is a selection of books on subjects related to the Molly Maguires:

Jules L. Bogen, *The Anthracite Railroads* (New York: Roland Press, 1927).

Richard O. Boyer and Herbert M. Morris, *Labor's Untold Story* (New York: Cameron Associates, 1955).

Wayland F. Dunaway, *A History of Pennsylvania* (New York: Prentice Hall, 1935).

James D. Horan, *The Pinkerton Story* (New York: G. P. Putnam's Sons, 1951).

Priscilla Long, *Where The Sun Never Shines*, A history of America's bloody coal industry (New York: Paragon House, 1989).

John O'Dea, *History of the Ancient Order of Hibernians and Ladies Auxiliary* (Philadelphia: Keystone Printing Co., 1923)

Marvin W. Schlegel, *Ruler of the Reading*, The life of Franklin B. Gowen (Harrisburg: Archives Publishing Company of Pennsylvania, 1947).

Irving Stone, *Clarence Darrow For the Defense* (New York: Garden City Publishing Co., 1943).

A History of American Labor (New York: Macmillan Co., 1959).

NEWSPAPERS

The Shenandoah Herald and *The Miners' Journal* (Pottsville) covered all aspects of the Molly Maguire story from 1874 to 1879. These newspapers also published verbatim testimony of most of the trials.

The New York Times, The New York Herald, The New York World, The New York Globe, The Philadelphia Inquirer and scores of other prominent newspapers covered the trials and executions.

191

By the same author:

Memories of Dungloe

• Memories of Dungloe, County Donegal, in the 1940s and 1950s.
  • An old Molly Maguire dies in Dungloe 70 years after the hangman claimed his brother in Mauch Chunk, Pennsylvania.
    • A German spy masquerading as a Dutch woman is arrested.
    • Many young men leave to go off to fight in the foreign wars and never come back.
    • Innisfree - an island paradise for children.
    • Protestants and Catholics - an uneasy coexistence.
    • Ghosts, superstitions and offbeat characters.

"A wonderful story that is well worth reading."
            - Angela Carter, Irish Books and Graphics, New York

Published by
P. H. Campbell
82 Bentley Avenue
Jersey City, NJ 07304
(201) 434-2432

$11.95